PATHWAYS *to* GREATNESS

for ELL NEWCOMERS

A COMPREHENSIVE GUIDE FOR SCHOOLS & TEACHERS

Michelle L. Yzquierdo

Published by Seidlitz Education
P.O. Box 166827
Irving, TX 75016
www.seidlitzeducation.com

For related titles and support materials visit www.seidlitzeducation.com.

12.17

Table of Contents

Dedication

My Bedstemor and Bedstefar along with my aunt and mom (far left) in July 1957.

This book is dedicated to Oscar William Redder (February 7, 1912 – December 17, 1985) and Ester Enggrob Redder (February 28, 1908 – May 24, 1994), my Bedstemor and Bedstefar. Your sense of adventure and big dreams sent you on your immigration journey to the United States. And to my aunt, Nini Redder Riggs, and my mother, Bente Redder Williams, who had to endure the challenges and adversities of being non-English-speaking secondary newcomers at a time when there was so little guidance, assistance, and support for students like you, thank you for the sacrifices you made and all the obstacles you had to overcome. I hope I've made all of you proud.

Acknowledgments

Thank you to my two loves: my husband, Carlos and my son, Kai. I could not do the work I do without your support, encouragement, and love. Thanks also to my fabulous in-laws, Josefina and Hector Yzquierdo, for all your help with Kai during the crazy hours of writing.

I would also like to express my sincerest appreciation to the Seidlitz Education team who supported me through this process and helped make this dream of a book come true. Special thanks to John for pulling such an amazing team together and for allowing me the opportunity to be one of them. I also want to thank Meg and Anna for helping me get the words out of my head and onto the page, and Anne-Charlotte for making my words look so beautiful.

Thank you to the talented and remarkable educators I get to work with who are a constant source of inspiration and ideas. Special thanks to my Pasadena ISD family for the feedback and friendship: Sarah Potter, Whitney Barber, Carrie Barras, Suzy Caballero, Ginger Ediger, Antonio Escobar, Nikki Lewis, Andrea Morgan, and Chris Puente.

And of course, thanks to all the beautiful children and former students who have touched my heart and enriched my life.

Foreword

I recently spent a day on a campus in Houston with ELL newcomers. They had just experienced Hurricane Harvey and its aftermath, and many of them had come here after traumatic situations in their home countries. They came from places as diverse as Iraq, Venezuela, El Salvador, Sudan, and Myanmar. Some were highly educated in their own countries; others had experienced interrupted formal education. These students' spirit and drive inspire me, and one student in particular stands out. His name is Ali. He left Syria when he was in third grade because of the war. He did not attend school until he was in Houston, beginning as a ninth grader. Right now he is on track to graduate.

But how was this possible? Is Ali's success story a fluke? Dr. Michelle Yzquierdo's surprising answer is "No." Ali's success tells the story of an incredible system of support within the school. His school has established a welcoming environment where culturally responsive teachers help all students feel valued and included, regardless of their language and background. Content-area teachers deliver lessons using sheltered strategies, the students receive focused, targeted English language development instruction, and the school has measures in place to help students rapidly acquire credit through creative scheduling.

Beginning with her work on her doctoral dissertation, Dr. Yzquierdo has been identifying the key elements of these systems of support that help students like Ali. She has worked with school after school where administrators and teachers are putting in the heart and the time to create support systems in which newcomers thrive. Now she is making a difference by sharing what works with other teachers and administrators.

This book, *Pathways to Greatness for ELL Newcomers: A Comprehensive Guide for Schools and Teachers,* puts into one user-friendly format the wisdom she has gained from all her work. It reflects her experience, first as a biology teacher teaching newcomers at a school in Pasadena, then as a specialist at a newcomer program, and finally as an ELL specialist and consultant working with countless schools serving newcomer ELLs. In the book, Dr. Yzquierdo details five critical practices we can implement for newcomer success: Know Your Newcomers, Construct a Culture of Care, Create Comprehensible Lessons, Enhance ELD Instruction, and Schedule for Success. Her book is rich in theory — yet practical by design. It allows readers to jump into which ever topic is most immediately relevant to their current work. What I think really makes this book useful are the specific activities and detailed instructions that help educators put these ideas into practice in their schools.

My suggestion to you, as a reader, is to take a look at the table of contents and start with whatever catches your eye. Share what you discover with your team, and help make Ali's success story become the norm. In working together, we can continue to make a difference for our ELL newcomers.

John Seidlitz

INTRODUCTION

How do educators use this book?

This book is meant it be a reference for you. If you are so compelled, please feel free to read it from cover to cover. If, however, there are certain sections that interest you more than others, I 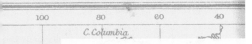 encourage you to go straight to those sections and read them first. Although the entire book will be a useful tool for you when developing your skills as a teacher of newcomers, it does not have to be read in the order it was written. Additionally, please don't be over-whelmed by the amount of content in this resource. If you are new to teaching or new to teaching newcomers, it may be daunting flipping through these pages, realizing there is so much to learn and get good at regarding newcomers. The fact that you are reading this book means you care enough to hone your craft, and that means a great deal. Teaching newcomers is a wonderful, amazing, rewarding experience, and you'll find your newcomer legs as you get more and more practice plan-ning and executing your lessons with them in mind.

How is this book organized?

I have chosen to write the book in a question–answer format. The purpose of this method is so the information can be presented in a clear and concise manner to avoid you having to sift through pages of text to get the information you want or need. Since the newcomer population can be very diverse, the first chapter, "Know Your Newcomers," describes the various populations of newcomers and newcomer characteristics. Chapter 2, "Construct a Culture of Care," details the very important concept of establishing a welcoming environment, developing cultural proficiency, and assisting students in overcoming culture shock. This is a very important chapter, and I encourage you to consider reading it first. Chapter 3 is a comprehensive guide to planning and delivering great lessons that are comprehensible to newcomers. If you are a content-area teacher with newcomer ELLs in your class for the first time, it is imperative that you familiarize yourself with the contents of this chapter. If you are an ESL or ELA teacher, Chapter 4, "Enhance ESL," will be useful to you. Content teachers, don't skip this chapter, however, even if you save it for

last. There is some information in here that will be useful to you, too. And lastly, Chapter 5 outlines all the logistical concerns regarding newcomers, including grade placement, scheduling, credits, and other programming concerns. The book wraps up with several appendices containing many resources for teachers of newcomers, including a fairly comprehensive list of recommended videos and books that is several years in the making.

Throughout the book, you will see a feature called Newcomer Voices (Johnson, 2013). These are stories from former high school students who were participants in my doctoral research. They were all newcomer ELLs who arrived in the United States as secondary immigrants and found their pathways to greatness.

FOR FABIO AND DIEGO, IT WAS THE CLEAR EXPLANATIONS OF ACADEMIC TASKS

they found most helpful. As Fabio explained, "I believe all my teachers did right because all of them would explain it the way I needed it so I could understand. They would explain step by step, really slow. I think that's one thing that has helped me out through all these years in math classes."

What are the current statistics for newcomers in the United States?

The immigrant population of the United States has been steadily rising over the last 40 years, from 4.7 percent of the total population in 1970 to 11.1 percent in 2000. Between 2000 and 2009, the immigrant population grew by an estimated 7.4 million people, bringing the total number of foreign-born individuals living in the United States to 38.5 million in 2009 (Grieco & Trevelyan, 2010). Immigrants and their U.S.-born children now number approximately 84.3 million people, or 27 percent of the overall U.S. population

(Zong & Batalova, 2017).These increasingly high levels of immigration are changing the demographic profiles of public schools throughout the United States. In fact, most of the increase in enrollment in the nation's schools can be attributed to a steady rise in immigration (Camarota, 2007). In 2000, for example, immigrant students accounted for 5 percent of the total population of students in pre-kindergarten through 12th grade, up 2 percent since the 1970s. This number increased to over 7 percent by 2010 (United States Census Bureau [USCB], 2010).

Newcomers by country, 2014

(Zong & Batalova, 2017)

INDIA 147,500

CHINA 131,800

CANADA 41,200

MEXICO 130,000

PHILIPPINES 41,200

Included in these numbers are children adopted internationally; in 2014, these numbered 6,438, with 2,743 age 5 or over (United States Department of State, n.d.).

Languages Spoken by newcomers

Among immigrants age 5 or older (Lopez & Radford, 2015)

Within the total population of immigrants in 2014, approximately 50 percent (20.9 million) of the 42.1 million immigrants age 5 or older were not English proficient (Zong & Batalova, 2017).

44% SPANISH
6% CHINESE (INCLUDING MANDARIN, & CANTONESE)
5% HINDI OR A RELATED LANGUAGE
4% FILIPINO TAGALOG
3% VIETNAMESE
3% FRENCH OR HAITIAN CREOLE
2% KOREAN

CHAPTER 1

KNOW *your* NEWCOMERS

"HELP! WE JUST GOT A STUDENT FROM VIETNAM *yesterday, and we have no idea what math class to put him in."*

"We welcomed a pair of siblings from China last week, and no one here speaks Mandarin! How will he ever understand the content in biology?"

"A new kiddo just arrived today from Pakistan with a transcript, but we have no idea how to read it or which credits we can give her, if any!"

"We just got a new student from Guatemala who speaks absolutely no English at all! In fact, we don't know what language he speaks!"

As an educator working with English language learners (ELLs) in various capacities, I have received many emails and phone calls such as these over the years. Although the countries, languages, and schools vary, the stories are similar. A new student arrives for his or her first day of school in the United States, and the school is inadequately prepared to receive that student. Even schools and districts with well-developed English-as-a-second-language (ESL) programs often find themselves insufficiently prepared to accommodate immigrant newcomers, who represent a wide array of languages and cultural backgrounds, arriving at the secondary level. This chapter will introduce you to the various newcomer populations and begin the discussion on how to provide appropriate emotional and instructional support to these students.

Why Newcomers?

Why do educators need this book about newcomers?

When searching for resources to assist educators in meeting the needs of ELLs, there is certainly no shortage of great material. Research has yielded a number of effective strategies to address the academic and cognitive needs of ELLs in general, and teachers can find abundant resources detailing these research-based instructional strategies and best practices. But what of newcomers, specifically newcomers at the secondary level?

Secondary educators in the United States are often unprepared to meet the needs of the increasing population of late-entering, older immigrant students who must learn a new language as well as content in an abbreviated amount of time in order to complete graduation requirements successfully As the number of foreign-born students increases, educators are seeking effective support to increase both content knowledge and language acquisition, especially at the secondary level, where new immigrant students are most at risk.

What is lacking in the repertoire of resources for ELLs is a systematic reference tool addressing the specific needs of the ever-increasing population of secondary newcomers in the United States. It is my hope that this book fills that void and provides educators with a user-friendly, thorough, and practical reference tool to use as the basis for beginning to formulate a program and a plan to meet the needs of the secondary newcomer population effectively.

The high dropout rates of secondary immigrant students are evidence that this particular population is not being adequately supported. Data trends are bleak and indicate an overall increase in the dropout rate of immigrant adolescents (Child Trends Data Bank, 2012). Academic success of immigrant ELLs is becoming an increasing concern for schools and districts as the achievement gap between these students and other demographic groups persists. Furthermore, retention of secondary newcomers is also an increasing problem as immigrants are much more likely to drop out than their native-born peers. For example, although foreign-born students comprise only 10 percent of the U.S. population, ages 16 to 24, they represent 25 percent of the drop outs in this same age category.

Why did I write this book?

I did not begin my professional life as a teacher of ELLs. In fact, I didn't begin my postgraduate career as a teacher at all. Immediately after college I was working in a federal job when I began to consider teaching as an option for a long-term career. Teaching appealed to me as a way to stay connected to and share my love and interest of science while serving kids.

My first teaching assignment was at a predominantly low-socioeconomic status, high-minority campus teaching biology and aquatic science. It did not take long for me to realize that many kids in my class were struggling to understand not only the language of the content, but basic English as well. Many of my students were limited-English speakers and/or immigrant students. Although my campus at the time was not was not focused on specifically serving the needs of this population, I gravitated toward these students. It did not occur to me until later that perhaps it was my own personal story and the story of my family that steered me toward a career committed to the success of this population.

My grandparents, Oscar and Ester Redder, immigrated to the United States from Denmark in 1955. My Bedstefar (grandfather) came first, working hard to earn the money to send for my grandmother, mother, and aunt. My mom and aunt entered public education at ages 11 and 14, respectively, as non-English-speaking students. There was little to no support for immigrant students in the 1950s, as the United States was deeply entrenched in the post WWII "sink or swim" educational policies of the time. With no

support in an educational system with little tolerance for non-English-speaking students, my mother and aunt struggled greatly in school. They often recount stories of the difficulties they had, remembering what it was like to be a foreigner in the place they now call home. Hearing stories of my mother's early experiences as an immigrant student made me much more empathetic to the plight of many of my ELL students.

After three years of teaching, I was given the opportunity to lead a new team created to better address the needs of our ELLs. I would lead the team and teach biology to the newcomer, non-English-speaking, immigrant ELLs as well as the native-born ELLs, with a cross-section of other students. Our team received extensive training with sheltered instruction strategies and was given additional planning time and resources to develop our skills as the newly developed English language development team.

Although the training we received often met the needs of many of our ELLs, it did not necessarily give us the tools we needed to effectively support our brand new kids— those kids arriving in the United States and enrolling in U.S. schools for the very first time as high school students with little to no English proficiency. Unfortunately there seemed to be an unspoken expectation that these students would not make it to graduation and would most likely end up dropping out. Why were only some newcomer ELLs able to find success? What could we as educators do to help them? I continued to reflect on these questions as I advanced in my career to become a peer facilitator and later an instructional specialist charged with establishing a newcomer center in another district. These questions would later become the focus of my dissertation.

My doctoral dissertation examined the factors contributing to the success of high school immigrants. I set out to find students who had immigrated to the United States between 2001 and 2011 (under the umbrella of the No Child Left Behind Act) and who were first enrolled in U.S. schools as high school students. These students had to have also completed all requirements to receive a U.S. high school diploma. Utilizing many of the contacts I had made over the years, I solicited names from teachers and administrators in several districts in my research area. Although I had lofty goals of including many individuals in my study, I simply could not find many students who fit my research criteria. Unfortunately, as the statistics indicate, there weren't many students who came to the United States as high school immigrants and managed to gain the language and content knowledge necessary to successfully complete graduation requirements. Five final study participants were located and were willing to share their stories with me. Through in-depth, personal interviews guided by a series of questions, my goal was to develop a multifaceted, comprehensive narrative of these students' experiences and determine the factors that contributed to or hindered their success as high school immigrants. What I learned from their stories is echoed throughout this book and featured in the "Newcomer Voices" sections.

One More Thought on "Why"

Individuals have individual needs, and I believe being able to identify these needs and address them is one of the keys to success for educating newcomer students. I have seen a small handful of secondary immigrants succeed in spite of the insurmountable odds they face. Unfortunately, I have seen far more of these students become dropout statistics. These students are capable of wonderful, amazing things given the right amount of support, nurturing, and advocacy. It is for that reason I write this book.

As mentioned above, teachers and schools are at varying degrees of preparedness with regard to effectively meeting the needs of ELLs with varying cultural and linguistic needs. Toward one end of the spectrum are schools and teachers, with the best of intentions and experience in teaching the general population of ELLs, who are often still falling short of the above goal for secondary newcomers. Their effectiveness in meeting the needs of these secondary newcomers is limited only by a lack of resources, experience, and comprehensive training explicitly for this purpose. At the other end of the spectrum are those teachers and schools for whom serving ELLs, much less newcomers, is an unknown. I hope they pick up this book with an open mind and find something useful to glean from it. Overall, it is my hope that this book and the research that went into it will assist educators in making a difference for the incredible children who sit before them, no matter the disparities in language and culture.

Newcomers' Unique Challenges and Strengths

What is a newcomer?

For the purposes of this book, the term "newcomers" refers to any newly arrived, immigrant English language learners who are in their first year of school in the United States and who are at the early stages of English proficiency. Beyond this broad description, the newcomer population is quite diverse, with varying degrees of literacy in their first language, background experiences, socioeconomic status, immigration stories, and exposure to English. The newcomer population may include refugees (p. 37), students with interrupted formal education (p. 22), unaccompanied minors (p. 41), gifted newcomers (p. 28), and newcomers with possible learning disabilities (p.34), among others.

Why is it great to teach newcomers?

The United States, to a large extent, is a nation of immigrants. Throughout the history of this country, people from around the globe have arrived in our country to begin a new life, bringing with them their stories, religions, customs, and languages. U.S. schools play an important role in helping newcomers and their families adapt and contribute as they integrate their way of life into American society.

Teaching newcomers is a wonderful, amazing, fulfilling experience! Yes, it can feel overwhelming those first few weeks, when all you can seem to do is smile, nod, and point. Or when you have a student who is so completely overwhelmed, sad, stressed and/or depressed there may even be tears (yours and theirs!). Relax, and take a deep breath. Regardless of the circumstances that brought these beautiful children into your life and your classroom, with love, support, and a great teacher toolkit, these kids can be successful academically and be an integral part of your classroom community.

How can I leverage newcomers' unique experiences?

Newcomers often come to the United States to escape hardship and strife that are unimaginable to their peers. With those life experiences comes an extraordinarily high degree of grit, perseverance, and resilience. Newcomer students and their parents often have very high goals and expectations for both behavior and academics. Some of my greatest allies in the classroom have been the parents of my immigrant students, who had worked very hard to give their children a better life and an opportunity to be educated here in the United States.

Culturally speaking, many newcomers come from countries where the sense of family, community, and cooperation is much more significant, and this too can be an asset in the classroom. Newcomers bring with them a host of other cultural constructs and experiences that may be different from those of the other students in your class. When students communicate with, listen to, and learn from peers who have experiences and perspectives different from their own, they expand their knowledge base and gain valuable intercommunication skills that are essential to success in their higher education, business, community, and social lives.

How does a newcomer's immigration status affect enrollment?

According to U.S. Supreme Court ruling *Plyler vs. Doe* [457 U.S. 202 (1982)], undocumented students have the same right to attend public schools as do U.S. citizens and permanent residents. Furthermore, undocumented students are obliged under state law to attend school until they reach a mandated age. As a result of the *Plyler* ruling, public schools may not deny admission to a student during initial enrollment or at any other time on the basis of undocumented status. Nor may they require students or parents to disclose or document their immigration status. School personnel, especially those involved in the student intake process, should be aware that they have no legal obligation or jurisdiction to attempt to enforce U.S. immigration laws.

TABLE 1.1. Documentation Status and Enrollment

As a result of the *Plyler* Ruling	
Inquiries	• Public schools may not make inquiries of students or parents that may expose their undocumented status. • Public schools may not ask for information with the purpose of denying access to enrollment.
Proof of Residency and Immigration Status	• Proof of residency within district boundaries may be requested, but inquiring into students' citizenship or immigration status, or that of the parents or guardians initiating the enrollment of the child, is not relevant to establishing residency within the district.
Birth Certificate	• A district may require a birth certificate but cannot deny enrollment based on a foreign birth certificate.
Social Security Number	• Public schools may not require social security numbers for students, as this may expose undocumented status. • Districts cannot deny enrollment if a family does not provide a social security number. • Students without social security numbers should be assigned a number generated by the school or district. • Adults without social security numbers who are applying for a free or reduced lunch and/or breakfast program on behalf of a student need only indicate on the application that they do not have a social security number. • Denial cannot be based on lack of a social security number.

How might a student's immigration status affect achievement?

Although undocumented children in the United States can attend public school, they are legally prevented from securing employment when they complete high school, obtaining most public assistance, or attending most post-secondary schools. Post-secondary education is often not an option to these students, either because they cannot enroll or cannot pay. The Illegal Immigration Reform and Immigrant Responsibility Act of 1996 has allowed some states to pass statutes that deny undocumented students eligibility for in-state tuition and scholarships, and in some cases, even bar them from enrollment at public colleges and universities (NCSL, 2014). Because of the lack of post-secondary education and employment opportunities, undocumented students frequently enter high school with little motivation to achieve, may give up easily, and often drop out (Gándara, 2005).

Undocumented students also face a constant fear of possible deportation of themselves or of family members. These students and their parents may be apprehensive of school or other government institutions, thus making it challenging for educators to plan school meetings, parent–teacher conferences, and other school functions.

What Is DACA?

Deferred Action for Childhood Arrivals (DACA; 2010) is an immigration policy allowing certain undocumented people who entered the United States as children and who meet several other guidelines to request consideration of deferred action for a period of two years, subject to renewal. Those eligible for DACA are colloquially known as Dreamers (named after the previous Development, Relief, and Education for Alien Minors Act, which failed to pass). This deferred action includes exemption from deportation for a specified length of time and a renewable two-year work permit allowing recipients to work and attend school. **DACA does not provide a path to citizenship (United States Citizenship and Immigration Services [USCIS], 2017).**

In order to be considered for DACA, individuals must file an application and several other documents, undergo biometric screening (fingerprints and photographs) and extensive background checks, and pay a $495 fee. The waiting period is four to eight months, and the process must be repeated every two years to renew.

DACA recipients are only eligible if they meet all of the following criteria (USCIS, 2017):

- They were under 31 years of age as of June 15, 2012.
- They came to the United States while under the age of 16.
- They have continuously resided in the United States from June 15, 2007, to the present.
- They entered the United States without inspection before June 15, 2012, or they are individuals whose lawful immigration status expired as of June 15, 2012.
- They were physically present in the United States on June 15, 2012, and at the time of making the request for consideration of deferred action with USCIS.
- They are currently in school, have graduated from high school, have obtained a GED, or have been honorably discharged from the Coast Guard or armed forces.
- They have not been convicted of a felony offense, a significant misdemeanor, or more than three misdemeanors, and they do not pose a threat to national security or public safety.

In September 2017, the Trump administration formally announced the end of DACA, leaving it up to Congress to create a viable, permanent legislative solution for those currently receiving DACA benefits. As of this writing, no resolution has been made.

Background Knowledge

What is background knowledge, and why is it relevant to teaching newcomers?

Background knowledge, also called prior knowledge, is all the bits of information, academic and nonacademic, that students have collected through their life experiences. All students, consciously and subconsciously, bring these bits of information to subsequent experiences. They use this stored information as a scaffold or framework onto which to attach new information. Background knowledge is a vital element in learning because it helps students make sense of, process, and internalize new ideas and experiences. In *Building Background Knowledge for Academic Achievement: Research on What Works in Schools*, Marzano (2004, p. 1) asserts, "What students already know about the content is one of the strongest indicators of how well they will learn new information relative to the content."

When newcomers arrive in our classrooms, they do so with a wide range of background knowledge and experiences. They may be experts in some areas that are virtually unknown to some of our other students, but they still lack academically oriented experiences. I once had a student who was very experienced at birthing calves but hadn't been to formal school in several years. Some newcomers flee war-torn countries and can personally relate to concepts such as tyranny, civil unrest, and other terms that are vague abstractions to our other students. And even newcomers who are well-educated in their home countries will lack experience and knowledge of American culture and history. Accessing prior knowledge of a given topic, tapping into and activating that prior knowledge, and providing some foundational information when background knowledge of a particular topic is lacking will be the keys to success for your newcomers.

What levels of background knowledge do newcomers have?

Some newcomers enter U.S. schools having received solid academic foundations in their home countries. These students are literate in their first language and need English-language development to transfer content knowledge learned in their native country to the classes they are taking in the United States. Immigrant students with formal schooling in their home country typically become proficient in English at an accelerated rate (Crouch, 2012).

Conversely, many immigrant ELLs enter U.S. schools with interrupted or limited education in their native country and have considerable deficiencies in their content knowledge. Students with limited formal schooling (LFS) or students with interrupted formal education (SIFE) are recent arrivals in the United States who have deficits or gaps in their school history. These students are typically three or more grade levels behind their same-age peers and may be pre-literate or illiterate in their native language as well. In addition to academic concerns, these students may be unfamiliar with the routines, standards, and expectations of school in general. Immigrant ELLs within this category, especially at the secondary level, experience particularly high dropout rates resulting from both the minimal amount of time they have been in the United States and the difficulty of speaking and comprehending instruction in English (Krebs, 2013). The following table (Short & Boyson, 2012, p. 3) summarizes the types of newcomers:

TABLE 1.2 Types of Newcomer Students

	First-language literacy	Grade-level content knowledge	English literacy development (compared to other newcomers)
Literate (full schooling)	Yes	Yes	Faster
Literate (partial schooling)	Yes	No	Average
Students with interrupted formal education (SIFE)	No	No	Slower at first

Note. Reprinted from *Helping newcomer students succeed in secondary schools and beyond,* by Short, D. & Boyson, B., 2012, p. 3. Copyright 2012 by Center for Applied Linguistics.

How can I assess a newcomer's background knowledge?

Upon enrollment, most newcomer ELLs are administered some form of language assessment, which may include an oral language proficiency test and an assessment of their reading and writing skills in English. The results of these assessments can be of value when determining a student's proficiency in English. Beyond that, there are a number of options for assessing newcomers' background knowledge, including the following:

* Review of previous school transcripts from home country

* School-/district-created assessment including basic math tests with little to no English, computations only, progressing in grade levels

* Intake forms (see examples next page)

* Manipulatives

* Computer programs

NEWCOMER ACHIEVEMENT PLAN

Name

Date

Parent/Guardian/Adult contact

Gender

Age

Language

Country of Origin

Translator

Observer

Results from state-
approved assessments

Other relevant information

COGNITIVE (1)

TASK	OBSERVATION	GOALS	RESOURCES
Ask student to sort cards by color.			
Ask student to sort cards by living/non-living things.			
Ask student to sort cards by number and alphabet.			
Ask student to sort cards by plants/animals.			
Ask student to identify/describe continents/oceans and other features of a world map in first language.			
Have student solve/explain (numerical) math problems based on grade level.			
Ask student to identify date on a calendar and time on an analogue clock.			

AFFECTIVE (2)			
TASK	OBSERVATION	GOALS	RESOURCES
Ask student about his/her school experience. Have you attended school? How many years of school have you attended? What do you do well? What difficulties do you have in school?			
Ask student: Who do you live with, and where do you live?			
Ask student: Which three people do you talk to often? What are they like?			
Ask student: What do you like to do when you are not in school?			
Ask student (after school tour/lunch): What do you see in school? In the cafeteria?			

LINGUISTIC (3)			
TASK	OBSERVATION	GOALS	RESOURCES
Ask student to spell his/her name in first language.			
Ask student to read in first language.			
Ask student to write a description of what he/she likes/dislikes.			
Ask student to tell or summarize a favorite story in first language.			
Ask student to describe his/her current knowledge and experience of English.			

What are characteristics and unique challenges of newcomers with high levels of background knowledge?

We must be careful to not assume that all newcomers lack knowledge of academic terms or concepts. Some newcomers are quite proficient in academic language in their home language, just not in English. Additionally, secondary students often arrive in the United States having completed courses in their home countries. The concern for these students is that they are often misplaced or mis-scheduled into courses for which they have received credit or that they have already completed in their home countries. Transcript evaluation and granting of credits (see pp. 156-164) becomes crucial for these newcomers, especially for older newcomers in high school who do not wish to repeat multiple courses upon arrival in the United States.

ELLs, especially those who are in their first few years in U.S. schools, can often be overlooked when students are identified for advanced courses and gifted and talented programs, particularly if tests are verbal or depend on teacher recommendation. Moreover, teachers of advanced courses, especially in math and science, should embrace their roles in providing support for ELLs who may be enrolled in their classes. There is a common misconception that ELLs do not belong in advanced courses or that teachers of these courses cannot and should not be expected to meet the linguistic needs of these students in these advanced classes. This is simply not true. In fact, given the necessary linguistic support, newcomer ELLs can be successful in advanced courses.

KARINA DESCRIBED HER RELATIONSHIP WITH MRS. MENDEZ, A TEACHER WHO WAS INSTRUMENTAL

in her success. "She was so nice!" Karina exclaimed. Mrs. Mendez knew Karina did not speak English well but would "point things out" and tell Karina exactly what needed to be done. Mrs. Mendez also encouraged Karina and another ESL student in her class to pursue AP classes because "she didn't want us held back, even though we didn't know a lot of English. She knew we knew the math." Through Mrs. Mendez's ongoing support and encouragement, Karina was able to complete pre-AP algebra II, pre-AP geometry, and an upper-level AP statistics course. With a warm smile on her face, Karina emphasized, "Just because of her, I took all of those AP classes, because she pushed me."

What are the characteristics and unique challenges of newcomers with low levels of background knowledge (SIFE, LFS)?

Students with interrupted formal education (SIFE) or limited formal schooling (LFS) are a small subgroup of newcomers, often refugees, characterized by disrupted schooling. These students may have attended school sporadically, if at all. They have gaps in their educational experience due to time spent moving between countries or time spent in refugee camps. Gaps of several years are not uncommon due to war, environmental disasters, civil unrest, or political instability. In some cases, they may have been denied access to education due to their gender, their ethnicity, or their inability to pay required fees. They may even be the victims of forced labor or military service. These students may have minimal schooling in their native language and low levels of literacy and numeracy. In some cases, limited literacy is a result of coming from a language background that has no written form.

Socioeconomic Status and Parental Involvement

What is socioeconomic status (SES), and how does a school measure it?

Socioeconomic status is a general measure used to identify people with similar economic, educational, and occupational characteristics. In schools, the number of economically disadvantaged students is usually measured by the number of students and their families receiving some sort of governmental assistance in the form of free or reduced-price lunches.

How might a newcomer's socioeconomic status affect achievement?

Aside from the educational implications, students who live in poverty are confronted with an insurmountable set of challenges unique to low-income families. These obstacles are related to both a lack of money and the numerous activities and responsibilities that low-income families have to face each day to survive. These challenges, generally unknown to middle-class educators, frequently prevent low-income students from meeting what may appear to be routine expectations (Gándara, 2005; Payne, 2003). Daily life is complicated by such things as lack of a family vehicle, lack of childcare or healthcare, no money for books or school supplies, and little if any disposable  income. Furthermore, poverty can have negative implications on a child's health and general well-being as a result of the psychological stress brought about by severely limited resources (Aud, Fox, & KewalRamani, 2010).

The poverty rate for immigrants and their children is nearly 50 percent higher than the rate for native-born Americans and their children (Camarota, 2007). There are a number of academic implications for low-income, underprivileged students as a lack of resources and low socioeconomic status (SES) have a direct effect on academic achievement

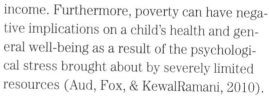

(Aud et al., 2010). For example, students with low SES and the same academic potential as their middle-class counterparts score worse on standardized tests (Gándara, 2005). This fact, along with the language and cultural barriers that ELLs must overcome, often leads to an underrepresentation of ELLs in gifted and talented programs, coursework focused on college readiness, and advanced academic and advanced placement (AP) courses. Access to these types of courses offers a variety of advantages to students, including preparation for college level course work and, in some cases, college credit (Klopfenstein, 2004).

What are the implications of parents' education levels on newcomers?

Parents' education levels have many implications for educators and schools. Primarily, the level of education attainment of parents often influences the motivation and achievement levels of students (Aud et al., 2010). Furthermore, higher levels of education reap numerous benefits, including a decrease in unemployment, less reliance on public assistance, and an increase in general health and well-being, among other things (Aud et al., 2010; Swanson, 2003). However, children of immigrants are less likely to have parents with relatively high levels of education compared to children of native-born parents (Capps et al., 2005). According to Capps et al. (2005), approximately 32 percent of immigrant parents with children in public schools did not have high school degrees. Furthermore, 15 percent of these parents had less than a ninth-grade education. Additionally, the number of parents of ELLs without high school degrees is even greater than that of the immigrant population.

Despite these bleak statistics, there are many immigrants whose parents have a high level of education that may not be reflected in their current employment status. However, it is the low education levels of immigrants that are a principal cause for the elevated rates of poverty in this population (Camarota, 2007). Additionally, schools with high levels of immigrant and ELL students may find it difficult to communicate with parents who may have relatively low levels of literacy in their home languages in addition to their limited ability to read or communicate in English (Capps et al., 2005).

How does parent support affect newcomer achievement?

Parental involvement in a newcomer's schooling can often be tied to cultural significance of schooling in the home country (Breiseth, 2011; Brewster & Railsback, 2017). For instance, in the United States, education and formal schooling are a highly promoted and cherished value. A myriad of opportunities exists for parents to be involved in school through parent–teacher organizations, parent volunteering, school picnics, bake sales, parent/grandparent breakfast and lunch get-togethers, and parent–teacher conferences. Such opportunities may be completely foreign to newcomer families.

Oftentimes a newcomer's parents' lack of involvement at school is misinterpreted as parents not being interested in their child's education. Depending on the country of origin, parents of immigrant students often hold the teacher and the school in such high regard that they will not interfere with either. Parents will keep their distance, deferring entirely to the authority of the school and the teachers (Breiseth, 2011; Brewster & Railsback, 2017).

A number of other factors exist that may contribute to the lack of parental involvement by immigrant parents:

- Lack of English proficiency
- Lack of knowledge of what interaction with the school is expected
- Lack of knowledge of what "school" looks like in the United States
- Lack of literacy skills in English and/or the home language, leading to very common situations of parents not being able to read the information sent home with the student
- Not enough time to attend school functions due to multiple jobs or small children to care for
- Lack of transportation
- Traditional gender roles prohibiting the mother from leaving the house or getting involved in school
- Undocumented status of parents leading to a fear of authority figures
- Parents being incompatible with people from other cultures
- Overall parental lack of knowledge with regard to decision-making authority when it comes to child education

Although not necessarily crucial for a successful newcomer program, parent support and involvement will greatly benefit your students.

JESÚS EXPLAINED HOW SUPPORTIVE AND ENCOURAGING BOTH HIS PARENTS WERE

regarding school and college. He pointed out that although his parents did not know the exact process or details of getting into college, getting financial aid, or applying for scholarships, they knew enough to constantly check on Jesús to ensure he was staying on track and meeting the appropriate deadlines. He told me, "They say, 'Hey, you already applied for the scholarship? You already applied for school? You already get in your classes?' They don't know the process, but they know what I need to do."

How can I promote parent support and involvement?

• Formulate outreach plans to meet and orient immigrant parents to the students' educational opportunities.

• Help parents become advocates for their children.

• Schedule home visits—families usually appreciate the effort and interest, and the dynamic among student, teacher, and family becomes more of a partnership, translating into more effective instruction.

• Help parents understand school routines and procedures.

• Let parents know what services the school offers.

• Translate school announcements and correspondence into the students' home languages whenever possible. If you do not have the resources to do so, look for someone who can communicate with the parents in their native language via a phone call.

• Seek out possible sources of bilingual interpreters, including churches, ethnic food stores, native language newspapers, local universities' international student organizations, other international community organizations and parents, and relatives of same-language peers.

• Invite parents, grandparents, siblings, family members, and neighbors to share their native culture in the class through songs, music, stories, pictures, special clothing, special dishes, and games.

• Organize a school cultural fair, and invite community members and family members to meet each other.

• Establish a family literacy night.

• Create a mentor program where second-year, third-year, and older students from the same or different cultural/language backgrounds mentor and support parents and families of newly arrived students.

• Be a community resource and advocate for newcomer parents—help them connect to community agencies, adult schools and resources and organizations that assist immigrant and newcomer families.

• Lastly, see newcomer families as an asset to the local school and community, and help them feel welcomed to the school and the country.

Quick tips for parent nights:

• Consider creating a carpool or arrange for transportation via school buses for parents who do not have transportation.

• Consider creating an area for child care for the younger children—use National Honor Society or Student Council members who are looking to volunteer their time.

• Offer a meal for parents and other family members attending.

Tips for Effective Home Visits

Traditionally reserved to address problems such as inappropriate behavior and poor academic performance, home visits are now seen as a valuable and highly effective tool in establishing and maintaining a strong parent–teacher relationship. Here's a list of other ideas you may want to consider in order to make home visits more effective (Crouch, 2016; Smith, 2016):

BEFORE THE VISIT:

Collaborate with colleagues

Before making home visits, teachers can collaborate with other teachers, administrators, and any other newcomer stakeholders to share ideas and information so that the individual making the visit can act as an ambassador for the rest of the team and share any pertinent information on behalf of others.

Address language concerns

With newcomers, the challenge with home visits is often the language barrier. Teachers who do not speak the student's native language can arrange for a qualified interpreter to assist. It's important to note that, whenever an interpreter is used, the speaker needs to look at the person being addressed and not the interpreter. If an interpreter is not available, simple words and phrases can be translated via Google Translate or a number of other translating websites. It is not ideal, but a smile and a few translated sentences let the parents know you care enough to make an effort.

Introduce Yourself

Make contact with parents/guardians (in their native language if possible) via email or in a letter sent with students. Introduce yourself, share your contact information, and explain the purpose of the home visit. For some immigrant families, a visit from school personnel may be a very odd thing. Some parents/guardians may interpret the visit as a sign of trouble. Emphasize that this visit is not to discuss misbehavior, poor grades, or any other negative aspect, but rather an opportunity to collaborate with them on their child's education.

Do your homework

Try to get to know something about the student's family. You might assign a project to students for them to provide background about their families that may include information about the parents/guardians, parents' careers, interests, and things the family enjoys doing together. This can be done via images and pictures (drawn, cut from magazines, printed off the Internet, etc.) and basic sentences. Do a little research about the student's home culture (pp. 49-53). Learning this kind of information about your students' families gives you great insights and provides speaking points when you meet them.

DURING THE VISIT:

Bring a gift

You can bring a small gift for younger children in the family or bring a gift for the house. This should be a small token of appreciation to thank them for meeting with you/welcoming you. Consider items such as children's books, coloring books, stickers, school spirit items, a small candle, tea, coffee, or a small treat.

Keep it positive

Even after hearing from you before the visit, parents/guardians may be reluctant to receive you in their home for fear that the visit is about something negative. Remind parents of your goal for a strong parent–teacher bond, and reassure them that you are visiting other students' families as well.

Be aware of cultural norms

Pay attention to your environment and the members of the family you are meeting. Be gracious. Accept offers of light refreshments, and try a little of each offering in order to show respect to the family. If everyone in the house is barefoot, take off your shoes. If everyone is finishing their beverage, snack, or whatever the family offered, you should too. Recall any pertinent information you learned from your culture research and apply accordingly.

FOLLOWING HOME VISITS:

Send a quick note or message

Reaffirm your commitment to a strong parent–teacher relationship, relay your contact details again, and thank the parent/guardian for their time and graciousness in welcoming you to their home.

Keep your word

Honor any commitments you made during the visit with the parent/guardian, and respond promptly to any future parent requests or concerns.

MANY OF THE NEWCOMERS I INTERVIEWED OVERWHELMINGLY RECOGNIZED THEIR FAMILIES as their primary source of support and strength. As Jesús described: "Even though we faced a lot of challenges, and even though my parents never knew the language and never knew how I was going to apply for college or how I was going to get financial aid for to pay my school, and even though sometimes we didn't have a way to transport me to activities in the school, they support me. They always were there, pushing me and challenging me and even though I always wanted to quit and just to get whatever job I can get, they always, always push me to do the best for me."

Learning and Intellectual Disabilities

What is a learning disability?

Learning disabilities are a generalized, umbrella category encompassing a number of other, more specific disabilities, such as dyslexia (disability in reading), dysgraphia (disability with written expression), dyscalculia (disability in math), and auditory processing disorder (disability with processing and making meaning of sounds), among others (Learning Disabilities Association of America, 2017; Understood: For Learning and Attention Issues, 2017). Learning disabilities are typically neurologically based processing problems that can interfere with learning basic skills such as reading, writing, math, spelling, reasoning, recalling, and speaking. These disabilities may also interfere with higher-level skills, such as organization, time management, abstract reasoning, long- or short-term memory, attention, coordination, social skills, and emotional maturity, depending on the specified disability. Generally speaking, a person with a learning disability is of average or above average intelligence and has a gap between the potential and actual achievement. Learning disabilities are lifelong challenges and are unrelated to a person's intelligence, motivation, or effort. Learning disabilities should not be confused with learning problems, which are primarily the result of visual, hearing, or motor impairments, intellectual disabilities, emotional concerns, or environmental, cultural, or economic differences.

What is an intellectual disability?

Intellectual disabilities are characterized by significantly impaired intellectual and adaptive functioning that adversely affects a child's educational performance. Individuals with intellectual disabilities may exhibit deficits in communication, self-care, and social skills, among others. Examples of intellectual disabilities include autism, Down syndrome, and cerebral palsy.

How do I know if a learning gap is the result of a disability or a language barrier?

Appropriate identification processes that can distinguish between a possible disability-related need and lack of English proficiency are crucial. Several factors that can potentially contribute to the misidentification of ELLs for special education services include: inappropriate and ineffective instructional practices, weak intervention strategies, inappropriate assessment tools, and a lack of knowledge of second language acquisition theory or understanding of cultural differences (Sánchez, Parker, Akbayin, & McTigue, 2010). Please refer to chart below from the resource RTI for ELLs (Seidlitz, 2010) for more details and clarification. Authentic and appropriate classroom assessments that help teachers discern whether a newcomer would benefit from an evaluation for special education services are a crucial component in the identification process.

TABLE 1.3 Characteristics of ELLs without/with a Possible Disability

ELLs without a disability:	ELLs with a possible disability:
SLA ability and progress is on par with linguistic and cultural peers	Student lacks vocabulary development even with rich language opportunities
Switches between languages during social and academic conversations	Struggles to communicate academic concepts in both L1 and L2
Exhibits skills involving interpretation of facial expressions and gestures	Appears to have difficulty interpreting and exhibiting facial expressions, gestures, and proximity to others
The gap of vocabulary development in native language is similar to the gap peers exhibit	The gap of vocabulary development in native language is significantly different from the gap peers exhibit
Student shows progress with linguistic support	Student fails to make adequate progress even when they receive linguistic support
Student remembers information recently taught	Student experiences difficulty remembering information recently taught
Failure to follow social norms is the result of lack of exposure to classroom routines and expectations	Failure to follow social norms continues despite sufficient exposure to classroom routines and expectations

Can a newcomer be assessed for special education services?

The Individuals with Disabilities Education Act (IDEA) and Section 504 of the Rehabilitation Act of 1973 address the rights of students with disabilities in school and other educational settings. To qualify for special education services, a student must have one of the identified disabilities under IDEA, and that disability must adversely affect his or her educational performance. Every school district has the legal responsibility to identify, locate, and evaluate students who are in need of special education services. If a newcomer is suspected of having one or more disabilities, the school must evaluate that student promptly to determine if a disability or disabilities exist and whether that student needs disability-related services. According to IDEA, disability evaluations may not be delayed because of a student's LEP or newcomer status. However, a student's limited English proficiency (LEP) status cannot be the basis for determining a disability. With regard to testing, if at all feasible, the special education evaluation should be provided or administered in the student's native language, some other mode of communication, and/or a form most likely to result in the most accurate information regarding the student's knowledge and abilities in order to determine whether a need stems from the lack of English proficiency or from a specific disability.

How are newcomers with disabilities served?

A newcomer's language-related needs as well as disability-related needs must be met. For these students, it is essential that the required Individualized Education Plan (IEP) team include participants who have knowledge of the newcomer's specific language and/or cultural needs, expertise in second language acquisition, and an understanding of how to differentiate between the student's language need and needs stemming from the disability. Additionally, steps must be taken to ensure that the student's parents understand the proceedings of the IEP team meeting. This may include arranging for an interpreter for parents with limited English proficiency and/or having the IEP, Section 504 plan, and related documents translated into the parents' primary language.

Refugee/Asylum Status

What is the difference between an immigrant and a refugee, and why is it important for me to know?

Immigrants come to the United States for a variety of reasons. Some come for educational purposes, others for employment opportunities, and some to join family members already living in the United States. Immigrants often plan ahead for their travels, selling their home and other possessions they aren't bringing with them, gathering important documents, making travel arrangements, and visiting with friends and family. The circumstances under which refugees leave their home countries, however, are vastly different. Refugees come to the United States to flee persecution, war, famine, and other dangerous situations. They often leave their homes quickly, with little preparation. They typically leave with few personal possessions or appropriate documentation and have little time, if any, to say goodbye to friends and loved ones. In fact, some refugees leave their homes not knowing the fate of family, friends, and neighbors. Additionally, while transitioning to a new country and resettling in a permanent home, refugees often live in refugee camps, which may lack even clean water and basic sanitation. Law and Eckes (2000) summed up the differences between refugees and immigrants in these poignant words: "An immigrant leaves his homeland to find greener grass. A refugee leaves his homeland because the grass is burning under his feet" (p. 7).

What is refugee/asylum status?

Individuals who have been persecuted in their home countries or have a well-founded fear of persecution can seek refuge for themselves and immediate family members in the United States under two programs: the refugee program for individuals located outside the United States and the asylum program for individuals already in the United States or at U.S. ports of entry. Once granted refugee/asylum status, the path is clear to legally enter or stay in the United States, work, and attend school. After one year refugees are required to apply for lawful permanent resident status, and after five years they may apply for citizenship (Mossaad, 2016; Pope, 2015). Upon entry into the United States, a refugee will receive a Form I-94, Arrival–Departure Record, from the inspector at the port of entry.

Who is eligible for refugee/asylum status?

According to 101(a) (42) of the Immigration and Nationality Act (INA), an applicant can be considered for refugee/asylee status if that person is unable or unwilling to return to his or her country of nationality because of persecution or a well-founded fear of persecution due to race, religion, nationality, membership in a particular social group, or political opinion. An individual must also be of special humanitarian concern to the United States, be admissible to the United States under the INA, and not be firmly resettled in any foreign country.

How is an individual granted refugee/asylum status?

An applicant meeting the above criteria can be referred to the United States Refugee Admissions Program (USRAP) under one of three priorities:

- Priority 1: individuals referred by the United Nations High Commissioner for Refugees (UNHCR), a U.S. Embassy, or certain nongovernmental organizations
- Priority 2: groups of special humanitarian concern
- Priority 3: family reunification

Less than 1 percent of the global refugee population is eligible to be assessed by the U.S. government (Pope, 2015). Next, a Resettlement Support Center (RSC), working in conjunction with the U.S. State Department, will conduct a pre-screening interview with the applicant and help complete the application for submission to the United States Citizenship and Immigration Services (USCIS). A USCIS officer will then conduct an interview to determine eligibility for resettlement in the United States. Several security checks will be completed before an application is approved. Upon approval, the refugee applicant will then submit to a medical exam. Individuals who successfully complete the process are assigned a sponsor and a resettlement agency, a private, nonprofit organization that assists the refugee applicant with housing, employment, and other services upon arrival in the United States. Before departure to the United States, applicants will receive cultural orientation lessons and must sign a promissory note agreeing to repay the cost of their airfare to the U.S. government within 42 months. Refugees are flown to the United States with the help of the International Organization for Migration

(IOM). The process for admitting refugees generally takes between 18 and 24 months (Westcott, 2015). Upon arrival in the United States, refugees receive services and support for a limited time from one of the national voluntary agencies that have contracts with the U.S. government (see Appendix A).

What are the most common countries of nationality for refugees and asylees?

In 2014 the leading countries of nationality for refugees were Iraq, Burma, Somalia, and Bhutan. Other countries of nationality include The Democratic Republic of the Congo, Cuba, Iran, Eritrea, Sudan, and Afghanistan. The leading countries of nationality for asylees were China, Egypt, and Syria. Other countries of nationality include Ethiopia, Iran, Iraq, Mexico, Nepal, Haiti, Guatemala, India, China, Egypt, Syria, Iran, Ethiopia, Haiti, Mexico, Venezuela, and Guatemala (Mossaad, 2016).

Who decides where refugees are resettled?

An assessment is made by a U.S.-based nongovernmental organization to determine the best resettlement location. Resettlement locations are decided on a case-by-case basis. Several factors are considered when selecting the new home for the refugee, including the location of other family members and/or friends of the refugee, location of an existing immigrant community from the same country, and the location of people who share the refugee's cultural background and language. Other considerations are employment opportunities, affordability of housing, and whether the community is willing and able to welcome the refugee. Additionally, any special health needs of the refugee will also be considered (Pope, 2015).

Where are most refugees resettled?

In 2014, more than half of all admitted refugees resettled in the following ten states (number in parentheses represents percentage of total refugee number for 2014): Texas (10.3), California (8.7), New York (5.8), Michigan (5.7), Florida (5.0), Arizona (4.2), Ohio (4.0), Pennsylvania (3.9), Georgia (3.8), and Illinois (3.7). The remainder of the refugee population was disbursed in the other 40 states (Mossaad, 2016).

What are the unique challenges of refugee students and their families?

Because of the devastating circumstances surrounding their departure from their home country, refugees must rebuild their lives from traumatic and tragic events. Moreover, refugees cannot safely return to their home countries and, therefore, will most likely experience a great sense of loss, sadness, and grief. Many refugee students have the additional emotional burden of being without their parents or other family members, who may be absent for a number of reasons, including death, detainment in the country of origin, or unknown whereabouts. In fact, research has shown that interpersonal trauma such as separation of children from their parents or adult guardian has a far more traumatic effect on a child than actual exposure to war (Masten & Narayan, 2012). Furthermore, because of limited resources upon arrival in the United States, refugee families will most often be living under extremely challenging and limited socioeconomic conditions. Refugee parents, like all parents, have a great deal of concern for their children. Refugee parents, however, often lack the personal, financial, or linguistic resources to effectively support their children in transitioning to an American culture and academic setting. The following summarizes other potential challenges of refugee newcomers and their families (Dryden-Peterson, 2011; Dryden-Peterson, 2015; Henyan, 2016).

MENTAL AND EMOTIONAL HEALTH CONCERNS

As mentioned above, refugee students may be experiencing severe stress and possibly even Post-Traumatic Stress Disorder (PTSD), a mental health condition brought on by experiencing severe trauma such as war, terror, or death, to name a few (American Psychiatric Association, 2013). Due to the extremely stressful circumstances typically associated with refugee status, PTSD is a legitimate concern for refugee students. Symptoms to be aware of that are relevant in an educational setting are:

- extreme daytime fatigue due to nightly sleeplessness and nightmares,
- inability to get along with others,
- paranoia and distrust,
- unwillingness to discuss life prior to the United States,
- persistent fear and anxiety,
- frequent irritation or agitation,
- difficulty concentrating,
- physical symptoms such as headaches, gastrointestinal distress, or dizziness, and
- suicidal thoughts or plans that may manifest in classroom drawings or writing.

Teachers should seek assistance from school or district mental health personnel if students or their family members exhibit any of these symptoms. More information about how to assist refugees who are suffering from severe stress, PTSD, or other mental health issues is available from the National Child Traumatic Stress Network (http://www.nctsnet.org/). The NCTSN offers many helpful resources related to the needs of refugee children and families. Additionally, KidsHealth in the Classroom (http://classroom.kidshealth.org/) offers a variety of free health resources, including teacher's guides, discussion questions, classroom activities and extensions, and printable handouts, that K–12 educators may find useful when helping students manage stress.

LACK OF DOCUMENTATION

Because refugees leave their homes quickly and with few possessions, student refugees and their parents often lack the important documentation needed for school enrollment, such as birth certificates, school transcripts and immunization and health records, to name a few. Many of these items are reproduced as correctly as possible and certified via the U.S. government resettlement process. School personnel, especially those responsible for school enrollment, should be aware of possible errors and omitted information on the reproduced documents. For example, birth certificates may have incorrect dates, and a student may be older or younger than the paper suggests. Additionally, some cultures do not place an emphasis on birthdays, and thus the date is unknown when the individual applies for refugee status. In these cases, the individual is most often assigned a birthday of January 1. This may cause confusion if there are multiple students with similar names and the same birthday enrolling in one school or district.

GAPS IN SCHOOLING

Refugees come to the United States having lived in temporary or unstable housing, such as refugee camps, for months or even years. As a result, student refugees (and perhaps their parents) may have significant gaps in their learning and may lack even basic numeracy or literacy in their first language. For older students at the secondary level, this can significantly affect their learning when they begin school in the United States. It is important to note that refugee students do not come to the United States completely lacking in background experiences, knowledge, and skills, as many teachers lament. Refugee students have experienced a world that most American students cannot imagine and, because of this, have developed skills in survival and decision-making, problem solving, resilience, perseverance, and grit. Because of their determination and fortitude, refugee students are more than capable of learning the academic and language skills necessary to be successful academically. It may just take longer than mainstream students or other newcomer ELLs who do not have the educational gaps the refugee students have.

WHAT ASSISTANCE IS AVAILABLE TO REFUGEES AND THEIR FAMILIES?

Because refugees arrive in the United States with little to no resources and oftentimes very few belongings, the federal government, in conjunction with the sponsoring resettlement agency, provides transitional assistance to newly arrived refugees in the first 90 days. The resettlement agency contracts with the Department of State to provide for the refugees' basic needs, such as food, housing, and medical care. The resettlement agency will also assist with employment, school enrollment, counseling, and other services that will help the refugee make a rapid transition to independence. It's important to note, however, that this initial basic support is not by any means comprehensive and often does not fully meet the needs of the refugee students and their families. For example, school supplies, money for field trips, supplies and materials for homework projects, and even appropriate clothing (e.g., winter coats in cold climates) may still be very hard to come by for these students.

What specific resources are available to help educators work with refugees?

Resettlement agencies have comprehensive websites with a great deal of information on various populations of refugees as well the assistance these agencies provide. This is a great place for educators to start when working with their refugee students. Additionally, the Office of Refugee Resettlement (http://www.acf.hhs.gov/programs/orr), a division of the U.S. Department of Health and Human Services, regularly publishes articles, videos, newsletters, and other resources on various refugee topics that educators may find useful. See Appendix A (p. 170) and Appendix B (pp. 171-172) for additional resources to assist you in meeting the needs of your refugee students.

Who are unaccompanied minors?

Over the last few years there has been a surge in the number of school-age children arriving in the United States from Central and South America (UNICEF, 2016). Typically these kids will not be documented, so they won't have the I-94 documentation that demonstrates or represents refugee status, but for all intents and purposes, these students have similar backgrounds to refugee kids. Unaccompanied minors often have large gaps in their background knowledge. They're travelling alone or with an older or younger sibling. They're often coming to the United States to reunite with their birth families or are leaving mothers and fathers behind to

come live with aunts and cousins. The journey to the United States for these children is often treacherous and traumatic, wrought with a great deal of danger and violence. Many of these children have had really traumatic and often violent experiences making that trip, including physical or sexual abuse, days without food, and other horrendous experiences. So a lot of these kids will have the emotional baggage and Post-Traumatic Stress Disorder that we see in other refugees. Many children and adolescents make this journey to escape even worse violence and poverty in their home countries and with the goal of reuniting with family who have come to the United States before them. Because many of these students have no immigration documentation upon arrival, they will not officially be designated with a refugee or asylee status. However, these students will have the same emotional and affective needs of refugee students.

ACTIVITY 1
20 Book/Article/Movie Challenge

Context:

Teacher/Self, Teacher/Teachers

Description:

The 20 Book/Article/Movie Challenge is meant to encourage teachers to continue to develop their CQ (cultural intelligence) by exploring various resources, including books, articles, and movies. One way to increase your expertise on a topic is by committing to read about it or watch movies and documentaries about it. The more you read about and explore other cultures with books and movies, the more your CQ increases. So what is the 20 Book/Article/Movie Challenge? It is simply a commitment to read or watch 20 books and movies/documentaries (I picked 20, but you can keep going after that) that will increase your CQ. Look no further than Appendix C on page 173 for the recommended books and movies list.

First, there are more than 25 movies from various genres as well as documentaries. I have seen every one of them, and I handpicked them because they either emphasize a certain culture or highlight examples of culture clash, ethnocentrism, or other timely issues related to culture and language. Many of the movies you may recognize. If you've seen them already, consider watching them again but through the lens of culture. I recommend starting with the movies and documentaries because you're likely to finish multiple films in the same amount of time it takes to finish one book. Besides, who doesn't like a good movie?

Next is a list of about 15 books on general cultural topics. Some of my favorite and most recommended books are on this list. Three in particular, *Material World, Hungry Planet,* and *Where Children Sleep,* will make wonderful additions to your classroom.

The remainder of the list consists of numerous titles arranged by geographical region that I have collected over the years. These books represent a spectrum of reading levels from children's books to books appropriate for middle and high school students. Most of these books can be purchased used online for a very reasonable price.

You can complete the 20 Book/Article/Movie Challenge by yourself or with a group of colleagues. I recommend the latter because I promise you will want to talk about these books and movies!

NAME _____

CURRENT POSITION _____   TOPIC/LANGUAGE _____

TITLE	AUTHOR	Date Completed

ACTIVITY 2
I Saw Myself

Context:

Teacher/Self, Teacher/Colleagues

Description:

This reflective activity is designed to help us connect with the experiences of our newcomers. "I Saw Myself" is a structured conversation with other teachers that helps us identify ways in which we have had experiences that are both similar to and different from those of our students (Seidlitz, Base, Lara, & Smith, 2016).

Directions:

1. Post the following stems in a clearly visible place during a team or campus meeting during which you are discussing issues related to your newcomers.

   - I am similar to_____ in that...
   - An experience I had in common with _____ was...
   - A goal I have in common with _____ is...
   - I wish I had been able to ___ for (newcomer)...

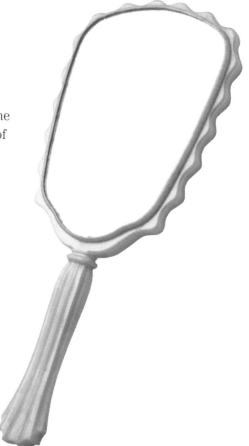

2. Have each person in the group write a response to one of the stems. Explain to the group that the purpose of the stems is to provide an opportunity to reflect on connections we have to our students and to try to understand our newcomers' experiences. The last stem enables us to think about a situation when we perhaps could have helped one of our newcomers, and yet we were unable to do so.

3. Share individual answers with the group. Discuss ways that we can help our newcomers realize that others have also faced the struggles they face and that we as teachers have a lot in common with them as people.

ACTIVITY 3
Strategic Survey

Context:

Teacher/Students

Description:

Many teachers struggle with finding ways to get to know their students and relate to them in personal ways. This activity focuses on using a student survey and checklist as a way of initiating positive relationships with students (Seidlitz, Base, Lara, & Smith, 2016).

Directions:

1. Create a survey with general questions about student interests, hobbies, and favorite activities to distribute to students.

2. Fill out one of the surveys yourself, and then distribute surveys to the students. Explain that the surveys are simply a way for those of us in the classroom community to get to know one another. Share your responses to the survey before having students fill them out. After students fill out the survey, have them share some of the responses with two or three other students in small groups.

NAME	I Found it interesting that
Anna	participates in Math Pentathlon
Charlie	plays guitar
Eli	bikes 7 miles to school
Kareem	plays football
Leo	enjoys reggae music
Marisela	wants to be an attorney
Matthew	plays chess

3. Ask the students, "Was there anything that you heard from one of the other students that you thought was interesting that you might want to share with the group?" Then allow students to share some of the things that they heard from some of their classmates.

4. Collect the surveys.

5. Create a chart with all the students' names in one column and a second column labeled "I found it interesting that... " (see example above).

6. Try to make at least one personal connection with each student based on the surveys or other information you hear about (from the school newspaper, announcements, etc.) and record that information in the right-hand column after you have had a short conversation with that student about that topic. For example, you might say, "Leo, on your survey you mentioned that you like reggae music. That is so interesting. How did you get interested in reggae?" Or, "Kareem, I heard yesterday you were released early to make it to the volleyball game. How was the game?"

7. Continue to review the checklist until you have made a personal connection with all of your students.

ACTIVITY 4
Beyond the School Walls

Context:

Teacher/Self, Teacher/Colleagues, Teacher/Students

Description:

This activity is an exploratory activity. It is possible to live in the same town or city but not be aware of the vast differences from one neighborhood to another. By stepping out from their home turf and into the neighborhoods where their students live, teachers have an opportunity to gain insights into and appreciation for the lives students lead outside of school (Seidlitz, Base, Lara, & Smith, 2016).

Directions:

1. Meet with colleagues and brainstorm a variety of ways to increase knowledge about the local community. The following ideas may be helpful:

   • Use the power of search engines to locate guides and maps of your community neighborhoods. If you are in a larger city or suburban area, there are sites to provide this information.

   • Spend some time in the neighborhood. If there are points of interest, visit them. Go grocery shopping and browse the area shops.

   • If there is a neighborhood newsletter or newspaper, get a copy.

   • If there are cultural events in the neighborhood open to visitors, consider attending.

   • Take pictures and/or videos of your explorations.

2. Share the results of your exploration with your colleagues.

3. Use the knowledge gained from personal exploration to modify activities and requirements in the classroom, and share any relevant pictures, videos, resources, and activities with your class. Examples:

   • Make direct references and connections to neighborhood facts during instruction. Show pictures or videos of your explorations to make a text-to-world connection for the students.

   • Have students speak with each other and to the class about their neighborhoods. They can make use of your photos or take their own. Provide sentence stems to facilitate their presentation.

   • Have students write (according to their proficiency levels) about your pictures. Writing could include captioning, describing, explaining, or comparing and contrasting. Beginners could offer their own drawings of their current or previous neighborhoods.

ACTIVITY 5

Measure for Measure

Context:

Teacher/Self, Teacher/Colleagues, Teacher/Self

Description:

One of the more challenging issues we face as teachers of ELLs is the extreme diversity we often encounter within our classrooms. We not only have ELLs, but also students who are gifted, students with special needs, students with reading disabilities, students with very little academic background knowledge, and students with a wide array of background knowledge and experiences. This activity is a means of structuring learning for ELLs and other populations of students in order to accommodate, differentiate, and assess their instruction. It takes into consideration the full measure of the diversity of our contemporary classrooms (Seidlitz, Motley, & Jones, 2011).

Directions:

1. Create a chart similar to the five-column chart at right. Begin by writing your students' names in the left-hand column.

2. Fill out the next column to the right, labeled "Proficiency Level," using the students' current English language proficiency rating or current teacher observations of each ELL's language proficiency level in class. You can use the summary of the language proficiency level descriptors found in the Appendix to help you assess ELLs' current levels of language proficiency in listening, speaking, reading, and writing.

3. Fill out the column labeled "Academic Background Knowledge" based on current teacher observation and conversations with students.

4. Fill out the column labeled "Language Ability/ Disability" based on each student's current IEP.

5. Fill out the column labeled "Learning Differences" based on students' IEPs and other information provided by your campus.

6. Use the information on the chart to help you accommodate, differentiate, and assess instruction for students.

Student Chart PERIOD_____

English Language Proficiency Levels
1 Beginner
2 Intermediate
3 Advanced/Advanced High
4 English Proficient

Academic Background Knowledge
1 Student with Interrupted Formal Education (SIFE)
2 Limited academic background
3 Standard academic background
4 Extensive academic background

Language Ability/Disability
RD   Reading Disability
WD   Writing Disability
SP   Speaking Disability
TD   Typically Developing

Learning Differences
AD   ADD/ADHD
AU   Autism Spectrum
GT   Gifted
TEN   Typical Educational Needs

NAME	Proficiency Level	Academic Background Knowledge	Language Ability/ Disability	Learning Differences

ACTIVITY 6
Every Student Has A Story

Context:
Teacher/Students, Student/Student

Description:
Every one of our ELLs has been successful at overcoming some serious challenges, both at school and outside of school. By providing a structure for students to share their stories and experiences, we can help them establish better relationships with their classmates and with us as their teachers (Seidlitz, Base, Lara, & Smith, 2016).

Directions:
1. Read and discuss a short story about someone successfully overcoming a challenge. Examples might include people such as Cesar Chavez or Malala Yousafzai.

2. Share with the students a time when you overcame a challenge. An academic challenge might be particularly helpful for students to hear about, or a challenge using a second language or one involving sports.

3. Ask students to write a short response to the following stem: "One big challenge I have successfully confronted is..."

4. Have students share their short responses with a partner and then describe their challenge in detail orally to their partner.

5. Have students write an essay about the challenge they successfully overcame.

6. Have students read their essays to a partner, then ask students if anyone heard from one of their neighbors a challenge that they think was interesting and that everyone should hear about.

7. Read the essays selected aloud, and then ask the students if anyone else would like to read their essay or have you read it out loud.

One big challenge I have successfully confronted is . . .

CHAPTER 2
CONSTRUCT *a* CULTURE *of* CARE

MOST OFTEN, NEWCOMERS TRANSITION into an academic and social setting that is vastly different than the one to which they are accustomed. This chapter will offer teachers, as well as all individuals who interact with or serve students, insights about culture that are imperative for understanding how to best serve newcomers. Understanding culture is the foundation for constructing and maintaining a culture of care.

Newcomers come to us from cultures that vary in their differences from mainstream American culture(s). For example, a newcomer immigrating from a Latin American country to a part of the United States where there is a large Hispanic cultural representation—as in the part of Texas in which I live—will find a number of teachers, fellow students, and community members with whom to communicate. That student may have access to Spanish-language television, radio, and other community resources, such as churches, grocery stores, and restaurants. If, however, the student is coming from a country that has no local representation currently in the new community—as is the case of many students immigrating from certain parts of Asia, the Middle East, and Africa—he or she will find the new community to be a completely foreign environment. These students will understand nothing of the spoken and written language around them, and they will be unable to communicate with teachers or peers. Constructing a culture of care will help welcome newcomers such as these to their new environment and ease the disorientation of being immersed in an unfamiliar culture, way of life, and set of attitudes.

Overcoming Cultural Barriers

What is culture?

Culture is the sum of social behaviors and norms that distinguish one group of people from another. Culture encompass such things as values, traditions, worldviews, social and political relationships, thoughts, feelings, attitudes, beliefs, and behavior patterns. These cultural attributes are created, shared, and/or transformed by groups of people with a shared history, geographical location, language, social class, religion, race, ethnicity, or social group, among other characteristics.

What are some aspects of culture of which I should be aware?

Because the United States is a diverse country influenced culturally by people from all over the world, it is difficult to compile a list of typical American cultural attributes. Nevertheless, the "Aspects of Culture" table on the next page shows several characteristics attributed to Americans by several combined resources. These American cultural aspects may be incongruent with the cultural beliefs and expectations of your newcomers. As new students immigrate to the United States and enroll in school, cultural clash is bound to happen. Additionally, newcomers will now be a part of and judged by a culture that they know little about. For example, in U.S. mainstream culture, promptness is rewarded and tardiness is considered to be rude or irresponsible

> ***TAKE NOTE**
>
> What seems logical, sensible, important, and reasonable to a person in one culture may seem irrational, silly, unimportant, and just plain ridiculous to an outsider.

behavior. In other cultures, however, time is a much more fluid concept with the idea of being "on time" varying by minutes or even hours. If your school has a strict no tardy policy, a student from Latin America, where time is a more fluid concept, may have difficulty adjusting to the idea that he or she must be in class by a specific time, with no exceptions. Rather than just assume the student should or does know this aspect of U.S. culture, engage this student in an explicit discussion of the need and expectation of being prompt. Any components of the "Aspects of Culture" table could be potential hotspots for cultural clash in the classroom or school. Knowing what some of these cultural aspects look like in the cultures of the students you teach can help assess and develop cultural sensitivity (see "Aspects of Culture" on p. 51).

TABLE 2.1 Aspects of Culture

ASPECTS OF CULTURE	MORE COMMON IN U.S. CULTURE	MAY BE COMMON IN OTHER CULTURES
Salutations	handshake	formal hugs, bows, handshakes, kisses on cheeks, hand pressed on forehead, sticking out the tongue
Communication and Language	explicit, direct communication; emphasis on content rather than context; meaning found in words	implicit, indirect communication; emphasis on context such as environment, body language, facial expressions; meaning found around words
Achievement	competitive; emphasis on results and success	cooperative; emphasis on nurturing, collaborative, supportive
Food and Eating Habits	eating as a necessity; fast food, more wasteful	dining as a social experience; religious and/or traditional rules; higher value placed on food as nourishment
Time	Clock time; precise times when events and appointments begin and end; value on promptness; time = money	Event time; times are approximate guidelines; relationship-oriented; events begin when needed people arrive; time spent on enjoyment of relationships; time is fluid
Age	value on youth; age seen as handicap; obsession with looking young	age given status and respect; aging process is celebrated, and elders are venerated
Interpersonal Conflict	preference for direct confrontation of conflict	preference for avoiding direct conflict; harmony preferred
Gender Roles	gender equality	different roles for men and women

*TAKE NOTE

Understanding another culture is a continuous, dynamic process.

What is ethnocentrism?

Ethnocentrism is common in every cultural group and is the belief that one's culture, or aspects of one's culture, is superior to others. Additionally, ethnocentric individuals tend to measure or judge others' cultures in relation to their own. Ethnocentrism is a natural proclivity of human psychology, and each of us demonstrates at least some degree of ethnocentric behavior, whether overt or subtle. For example, if someone were to ask you who the best college football team is, there is no doubt that most of you would vehemently defend the honor of your alma mater (Go Texas Aggies!). We also see ethnocentric beliefs manifest in state and national pride. Most Americans would probably declare the United States the best country in the world, and just ask anyone from Texas about which state is the best. Although ethnocentric views can be relatively harmless, allowing ethnocentrism to color your outlook on others outside your cultural group can have dire consequences.

When does ethnocentrism become harmful?

It is important to stay honest and open with yourself and monitor your thoughts, behaviors, and interactions with your various students for signs of more negative forms of ethnocentrism. For example, do you have the same expectations for your various students regardless of their race, sex, national origin, socioeconomic status, religion, or even where they live? I recall a comment by one of my colleagues very early in my educational career. She was lamenting about the influx of "apartment kids" we would soon be getting, implying that living in an apartment automatically equated to having behavior problems or not performing to the same academic standards as those from middle-class neighborhoods. When I pointed out that I grew up in an apartment and was one of those "apartment kids" she was now complaining about, *she assured me that I was different*. To what degree, I am not sure. I did not ask and quickly realized that I would not be changing her preconceived bias toward "apartment kids" even though I seemed to be the exception to her rule.

Have you ever found yourself to be an *exception to the rule*, as I was told I was? Who is to say that any or all of your students will not be the exception to the rule? Who says it's a rule? And for that matter, who made the darn rule?! Keeping an open mind and being truly unbiased in your expectations for your students will allow you to better serve their specific needs and promote their achievements equitably.

What is culture clash?

Culture clash or cultural conflict occurs when different cultural values and beliefs are in opposition to each other. Your cultural perspective or lens stays with you wherever you go. If you have ever traveled to a foreign country, you may have found yourself trying to apply your cultural lens to your new surroundings only to find the two were quite different. Others may have judged your behavior as rude or even inappropriate, or conversely, you may have been confused or put off by an individual's behavior toward you. These are all examples of culture clash. As an educator teaching a diverse group of students, you and your students have most likely experienced culture clash to some degree both inside and outside the classroom.

How can I overcome ethnocentrism and deal with culture clash?

One of the first steps in supporting your newcomers is to acknowledge any biases or ethnocentric views you may have. This is not always easy and may take some honest self-reflection and internal discourse. Be empathetic, open, and flexible and demonstrate caring for all your students' well-being and differences. Next, work on developing your cultural intelligence (CQ), your ability to relate to and work effectively across cultures. This can be accomplished by learning about the culture of your students and identifying possible scenarios where culture clash may occur (see 20 Book/Article/Movie Challenge, p. 42). If you have many diverse students from a multitude of backgrounds, it will be extremely difficult and time-consuming to gain in-depth knowledge of all your students' cultures. But as a minimum, a basic understanding of your students' varying cultures is a must. Cultural sensitivity, or knowledge, awareness, and acceptance of other cultures, will go a long way toward creating an environment that is nurturing and welcoming for your newcomers. Consider getting to know aspects of both the surface culture and deep culture of your students. Table 2 lists several aspects of each that may be relevant in an educational setting.

TABLE 2.2 Aspects of Surface and Deep Culture

Aspects of Surface Culture	Aspects of Deep Culture
Arts: music, visual, and performing arts	Relationships: how an individual regards his or her family, friends, classmates, and others
Holiday celebrations: patriotic, religious observations, personal rites, and celebrations	Folk myths: beliefs in traditional stories and superstitions (This came up a great deal in my culturally diverse biology classroom.)
Food and drink: food and culinary contributions	Gestures and body language: nonverbal communication, such as the use of the eyes, the hands, and the body
Folklore: folk tales, legends, and oral history	Role of age and sex: how an individual regards members of the opposite sex, older people, peers, and younger people
	Appearance and grooming: hair styles, use of cosmetics, dress, personal hygiene, etc.
	Rewards and duty: attitudes toward motivation, merit, achievement, and personal and social obligation
	Religion: attitudes toward and behavior resulting from the belief of the divine and/or supernatural
	Concept of time: definition of being early, on time, or late
	Ceremony: what a person is to say and do on a particular occasion
	Other values: attitudes toward education, fairness, competition, etc.

What is the Cultural Proficiency Continuum?

The Cultural Proficiency Continuum (below) represents a range of values, behaviors, and attitudes of an individual or organization reflecting their response to diversity (Cross, Bazron, Dennis, and Isaac, 1989; Lindsey, Nuri-Robins, and Terrell, 2009). As your cultural intelligence and cultural sensitivity increase (see previous question), you will move toward cultural proficiency on the continuum, which is the the ideal stage for teachers of newcomers.

TABLE 2.3 Cultural Proficiency Continuum

Stage	Description	Examples	What it Might Sound Like in School
Cultural Destructiveness "See the difference; stomp it out."	Using one's power to eliminate the culture of another	-Genocide or ethnocide -Exclusion laws -Holocaust during WWII in Europe -Bureau of Indian Affairs Schools in the early 20th century	-"When we re-district we can get rid of that neighborhood!" -"This is America. I wish they'd learn English." -"There are so many problems coming from those kids." -"If we could get rid of the special needs students, our scores would improve."
Cultural Incapacity "See the difference; make it wrong."	Believing in the superiority of one's own culture and behaving in ways that disempower another's culture	-Disproportionate allocation of resources to certain groups and lowered expectations for others -Jim Crow laws in the American South during the 20th century -Tokenism (hiring one or two individuals of minority groups to prove that the organization is open and inclusive)	-"Another generation to never leave the trailer park." -"He's _____ so we can't expect him to do much better than that." -"This is pre-AP. We can't have any ELLs in here."
Cultural Blindness "See the difference; act like you don't."	Acting as if cultural differences do not matter or as if there are no differences among/ between cultures	-Discomfort in noting difference -Beliefs or actions that assume the world is equally fair to everyone and achievement is based on merit only -Acting as if the cultural differences that you see do not matter, or not recognizing that there are differences among and between cultures -Belief that we are living in a post-racism world	-"Our school does not need to focus on multicultural education. We treat everyone the same." -"Everyone learns the same." -"Just don't recognize their religion. We don't want to offend." -"I'm not prejudiced. I don't even see color in my students." -"Aren't all Asian cultures the same anyway?"

Stage	Description	Examples	What it Might Sound Like in School
Cultural Pre-Competence "See the difference; respond to it inadequately."	Limiting beliefs to possible stereotypes about a person's or group's cultural practices	-Serving a soul-food meal during Black History month to demonstrate cultural proficiency -Lower expectations for certain groups	-"Diversity is covered through our language arts curriculum." -"Let's ask Ms. Rodriquez (the only Latina teacher in the school, who is actually from Costa Rica and not Mexico) to lead the Cinco de Mayo program." -"Make sure you do at least one activity for Black History month."
Cultural Competence "See the difference; understand the difference that difference makes."	Accepting and respecting differences	-Ongoing self-reflection regarding culture -Ongoing education of self and others regarding culture	-"You are you. I am me. But together, we are we." -"I think it is interesting to look at another's perspective through a different lens." -"Our school's mission statement capitalizes the word ALL, and we mean it."
Cultural Proficiency "See the difference; respond positively. Engage and adapt."	Seeking out and celebrating diversity	-Empathy and alliance for groups other than one's own -Interacting effectively in a variety of cultural groups -Having the capacity to teach and learn about differences in ways that acknowledge and honor all the people in the groups they represent -Advocacy, support, and modeling	-"With the addition of _____, our classroom experience has become richer." -"I'm so excited to have that new student from _____! The other students are learning so much from him." -"We need to look at our policy concerning _____. It is not very inclusive. Let's talk about ways we might change it."

Individuals in the proficiency stage of the continuum possess the five essential elements of cultural proficiency. Culturally proficient individuals do the following effectively:

- Assess culture: identify the cultural groups present
- Value diversity: develop an appreciation for the differences among and between groups
- Manage the dynamics of difference: learn to respond appropriately to the issues that arise in a diverse environment
- Adapt to diversity: change and adopt new policies and practices that support diversity and inclusion
- Institutionalize cultural knowledge: drive the changes in the system and help establish the new status quo

What is culture shock?

As an individual moves from one culture to another, he or she may experience what is known as culture shock. Feelings of apprehension, loneliness, and a lack of confidence are common when newcomers relocate to the United States and begin adapting to a new culture. Although culture shock is a profoundly personal experience and does not affect individuals in the same way, culture shock can be divided into five fluid stages (Pedersen, 1994). The table on the facing page summarizes the various stages of culture shock.

How can I support my newcomers as they overcome culture clash and culture shock?

There are several things to keep in mind when working with students who are experiencing culture shock. Primarily, overcoming culture shock is a fluid, dynamic process and not a single event or even a sequence of finite, fixed steps. Bad days can cause students to revert to a previous stage, and some students may go back and forth between stages a number of times before moving on. This is a normal part of the process. Furthermore, some stages may be skipped altogether. For example, some newcomers may never experience the honeymoon stage and will skip right to the fear, apprehension, sadness, and anger of the disintegration and reintegration stages. I have known many students like this, whose harrowing stories of just getting to the United States caused so much trauma that they never experienced anything except profound fear and sadness. These students needed a great deal of love, support, and caring from devoted teachers to even make it through the day. The light at the end of the culture shock tunnel is that overcoming this critical aspect of immigrating to the United States teaches our students an entirely new set of coping strategies that will contribute to their future success.

JESÚS FURTHER CHARACTERIZED HIS TEACHERS:

"They knew that you don't know the process, but they wanted to push you because the staff saw something that you didn't see within yourself. They pushed you because they saw what was within yourself."

TABLE 2.4 Stages of Culture Shock

	In this stage of culture shock...
Honeymoon Stage	...the newcomer will find the new culture and his new life in the United States intriguing and exhilarating. This stage can last anywhere from a few days to a few weeks. It is characterized by feelings of excitement, euphoria, anticipation, and eagerness as everything and everyone is new and exciting.
***Disintegration or Distress Stage**	...newness and excitement of the situation begin to diminish, and those initial euphoric emotions are replaced with anxiety and depression. The newcomer begins to feel confused, isolated, and inadequate as he struggles in the new environment, often without the usual support of friends and family.
***Reintegration Stage**	...negative thoughts and feelings escalate to anger and sometimes despair as the newcomer experiences a constant inability to function. She may stay in a continuous state of frustration, showing signs of hostility toward the United States and aspects of U.S. culture such as the food, people, and language.
Autonomy Stage (Also known as adjustment, recovery, or emergent stage)	...the newcomer becomes more familiar with her new home and begins to adjust accordingly. She becomes more comfortable with the culture, people, food, and language and feels less homesick. Feelings of isolation diminish as the newcomer makes new friends and begins to establish a support system here in the United States. She is better able to handle situations that were previously frustrating and grows much more confident in navigating the new culture.
Independence Stage (Also known as the acceptance stage)	...the newcomer begins to appreciate the similarities and differences between his home country and the United States. He feels less and less like a foreigner and begins to see the United States more like home—or at least a second home. Feelings of success grow as the newcomer becomes more and more bilingual and bicultural. He is now comfortable, confident, and no longer alone or isolated.

*The disintegration and reintegration stages can last indefinitely.

*Other signs of these two stages may include sadness, extreme homesickness, exhaustion, constant worry, and overeating/weight gain.

*Recognizing the signs and symptoms of the disintegration and reintegration stages in your newcomers can help you reassure students that these emotions are normal and expected. Furthermore, with a great deal of love, support, and empathy, you can help students move through these two stages and on to the autonomy and independence stages.

What are some ways I can create a welcoming environment in my classroom?

- Establish high expectations for all your students, and help the students see their developing biculturalism and bilingualism as an asset and not a hindrance.

- Provide books and magazines in the students' native languages. This is especially important in a language arts class, where students are given the opportunity for free reading. Students greatly benefit from having access to native-language materials so they can continue to strengthen literacy in their first language, especially at the beginning of the English acquisition process when English reading skills will be severely limited.

- Display maps, flags, and other symbols from the students' home countries, and use them in class. Students can add pins to the map indicating their countries of origin. Each country of origin can also be represented by hanging a flag from that country. And, lest you think the cost of all these flags will be pricey, one of my favorite examples of this was from a middle school teacher who made all her flags from construction paper. Better yet, consider this a great beginning-of-the-year icebreaker activity for your class.

- Decorate the room with other culturally representative items, such as posters, pictures, and calendars in other languages and mementos that represent various countries and cultures.

- Celebrate students' various cultural holidays. This doesn't have to take away from valuable instructional time. Simply acknowledging the holiday for the student will go a long way toward letting him know you cared enough to learn a little about his culture. It might sound a little like this: "Class, before we begin our lesson on biomes today, please join me in wishing Anh a happy New Year. Anh, would you like to tell us a little about this holiday and how it's celebrated in your country?" Consider that if this student were still in his home country, this particular day would hold a great deal of significance for him and would most likely be celebrated by the whole family.

- Incorporate multiculturalism and diversity into your lessons whenever appropriate.

- Attend local cultural events in your students' neighborhoods or churches, and eat at local ethnic restaurants frequented by your students and their families. Talk to your students about where and when these events might be taking place. You will learn more about them and their culture while also sending the message that you are interested in getting to know them beyond the classroom— a crucial aspect of lowering the affective filter (see Chapter 3 p. 79).

- Have students create family histories by interviewing older family members and neighbors, and invite them to share the information with the class

- Create and post a class motto, chant, and/or goals. Post and review these daily with your students. The following is an example from Ms. Bizati's class at Fondren Middle School in Houston Independent School District:

ALL OF THE STUDENTS EMPHASIZED THE IMPORTANCE OF HAVING ENCOURAGING TEACHERS

with high expectations. Fabio explained: "[My teacher] doesn't treat us like we can't do things. She treats us like we can do things. If you don't know, you can learn. She was hard because [she] had to be expecting things. That doesn't mean you have to be mean. That doesn't mean you don't care. That doesn't mean you only care about work. She is a great person."

Fabio also pointed out, "I knew [the teachers] cared because I knew they pushed me to do things for myself." He continued: "I was taking English Four and got Ms. Stounch. Oh my God, she's awesome. She really, really cares about us. She was giving me the exam that we had to take to get out of high school. She would give us [standardized testing] tutorials. She was really awesome. She would tell us how to answer the questions, how to read the passages, how to make your essay, all of that stuff. She was really into helping us.

"WE ARE GLOBAL LEADERS!

WE PUSH THROUGH OUR STRUGGLES BECAUSE WE STRIVE FOR EXCELLENCE!

WE ARE PROUD OF WHERE WE COME FROM BECAUSE THAT MAKES US WHO WE ARE TODAY, TOMORROW, AND BEYOND!"

This mission statement is prominently posted in Ms. Bizati's class, and each day begins with a rather loud and enthusiastic recitation of the mission statement led by a student volunteer. In fact, this statement and the class goals are some of the first things newcomers learn in English in Ms. Bizati's class.

What are some ways the school can create a welcoming environment for newcomers?

Many of the above ideas can be implemented school-wide. Maps and flags representing countries of origin can be displayed in the front office and throughout the building. Acknowledgment of holidays can be included in daily or weekly announcements and parent newsletters. Additionally, consider the following ideas:

- Provide visual cues (arrows, footprints, etc.) throughout the building so that newcomers and their families can readily navigate to desired locations. This is especially important in large buildings or buildings with confusing layouts. Consider the ease of locating the following in your building: front office/administration, nurse, cafeteria, restrooms, attendance, any buildings or rooms off the main building, and any other locations that might be needed. Now consider the above through the eyes of a newcomer or the family of a newcomer who may have very limited English proficiency. Do the navigational cues in your building, if you have any, rely heavily on signs with text, or do they also include pictures, symbols, or other nonlinguistic supports?

- Properly prepare reception staff in your building to greet new immigrant students and families, emphasizing the power of body language and facial expressions along with patience, compassion, and sensitivity when verbal communication is not an option. Offer mini training sessions for other teachers, school personnel, and even other parents and students to get to know each other's customs and cultural values. Additionally, many of the ideas in this book could be shared with all staff, including the section on culture clash, ethnocentrism, and aspects of culture.

JESÚS MADE IT CLEAR THAT SCHOOL PERSONNEL WERE ALWAYS AVAILABLE TO HELP

when he needed it. "People were there asking us if everything was fine and would be there if I, or if we, had a question. My teachers, even the teacher aides, they were there. Even the other students were there. Sometimes I would say, 'I don't know English, I don't know their language, I miss being home [in Mexico].' Because it was hard to call [the United States] home when you feel like a stranger. So the staff members, even though they did not know [Spanish], they always knew who to refer you to. You can feel comfortable talking in your language. That was just something. That really was helpful that the people were there and they lent you the books, they lent you the dictionaries if you needed them."

DIEGO TOLD ME ABOUT HAVING TROUBLE NAVIGATING HIS NEW, MUCH LARGER,

U.S. high school during his first few days. "I still remember I had some trouble finding all the classes because everything is so different from Mexico. Over here, you have a teacher and a classroom for each class. Over there you just stay in one classroom, and the teachers come to you. You just stay there the whole day."

Who are the newcomer stakeholders, and how can they work together to support newcomers?

The organization of the school is a contributing factor to the achievement of secondary ELLs and newcomers (Ruiz-de-Velasco, Fix, & Clewell, 2000). Standard practice in the United States is to partition the secondary school into departments and isolate the teachers by these departments. Furthermore, the school day is often divided into isolated, finite blocks of time with very little cross-curricular dialogue or discourse. These practices lead to a "your kids" mentality where only certain teachers and staff are expected to see themselves as part of the ELL/newcomer team. This role separation is ineffective in addressing the language acquisition, instructional, or affective needs of newcomers. In addition to mainstream teachers, counselors and administrators should be part of the team when developing and implementing a successful newcomer plan (Gándara, 2005; Lee & Avitia, 2008).

The following groups of people are who I call "newcomer stakeholders." They each play a critical role in making sure that newcomer ELLs feel welcome and integrated into the school system. You can read more about

newcomer programs on p. 165. In addressing the affective needs of our learners, we help them on their pathway to success, both within and beyond our schools and classrooms.

Administrators

Administrators are essential to newcomer success. In addition to the "standard" job description, the administrator is entrusted with overseeing the ESL/newcomer program, mentoring and supervising teachers, and allocating funding and resources. The administrator, like the teacher of newcomers, should have a deep knowledge of culturally and linguistically responsive instruction as well as knowledge of students' cultural backgrounds. The administrator is encouraged to use that knowledge to promote cultural and linguistic competence campus-wide.

Counselors

Counselors are of particular value when planning and implementing a successful ESL program, as they can provide a broad range of services and personalized attention that are crucial for ELL success (Crouch, 2012). Counselors oversee schedules, grant credits, and provide access to advanced coursework,

NEWCOMER VOICES

ANOTHER SCHOOL EMPLOYEE FROM WHOM KARINA FOUND A GREAT DEAL OF HELP

and support was her counselor, Ms. Dorals. Karina met Ms. Dorals the day she and her family came to register Karina for high school. Karina explained that Ms. Dorals was very kind to her and "held my hand all my high school years." Ms. Dorals acted as a sort of case manager for Karina, monitoring her coursework, credits, and progress throughout high school, seeing that she took the appropriate classes, and assisting her with getting into summer school so that Karina would have the room in her schedule for the upper-level math classes she wanted to take. Karina told me that she always understood everything Ms. Dorals said because Ms. Dorals always spoke very slowly and clearly and made it a point to talk to Karina and, as Karina expressed, "She was always very, very patient with me."

and they also educate newcomers about various post-secondary opportunities and career options that are often not emphasized for secondary ELLs (Crouch, 2012; Lee & Avitia, 2008). Crouch shed light on the fact that many successful ESL programs have utilized counselors in a case manager capacity. These case managers built prolonged relationships with the ELLs, closely monitored each student's attendance and academic progress, and provided interventions as needed in a timely manner. The counselors also assisted the students' families in overcoming barriers to the students' educational success.

Instructional support personnel and noninstructional personnel

Instructional support personnel and noninstructional personnel also play an integral, and often overlooked, role in newcomer adjustment and achievement. However, these individuals are seldom included in staff development and training specific to this population.

Bus drivers

Drivers can be made aware of the importance of positive body language and facial expressions, and how these nonverbal cues are essential when oral communication in a common language is not possible. Ensure that drivers also have a list of the newcomer students who will be riding their buses along with other information, where applicable. Information such as the home language of the student, the student's address, perhaps a picture, and any other pertinent cultural information may be useful. For example, drivers may be told that a child comes from a culture in which eye contact between children and adults is considered taboo. Additionally, drivers can be encouraged to contact the school with information regarding upcoming safety drills so the school can take steps to inform the student and/or the student's family that such a drill will be occurring. Imagine how frightening it would be for a newcomer to be on a bus during an evacuation drill, not knowing the drill is for practice only.

During my interview with my former student Karina, she recalled an extremely traumatic experience she encountered the first day she rode the school bus home from school, which brought her to tears as she conveyed the story to me:

AFTER THE FIRST DAY OF CLASS, KARINA WAS TO RIDE THE BUS TO A NEARBY STOP

on Alabama Street and walk the rest of the way to her aunt's home, where she and her mother lived. The entire summer before school, Karina, with the help of her aunt, familiarized herself with neighboring streets in the unlikely event she got off at the wrong stop. Karina explained, "If I get off anywhere around here, I know where to go."

On this particular day, Karina saw the name of the street, Alabama, from her bus seat. She got up from her seat to get off the bus but realized that nothing looked familiar. Karina hesitated. The driver inquired as to which street was Karina's stop, and when Karina told him "Alabama," he insisted that she was in the correct place and made her get off the bus. Karina recalled the driver saying, "This is your street. There are so many kids that need to be dropped off, so you need to get off the bus." Karina could understand the driver but did not have enough English proficiency to explain to him that she was unsure about getting off the bus at that particular location. It would be over two hours before Karina found her way home.

As Karina relayed the details of this particular event, her voice got shaky, and tears filled her eyes. Obviously still traumatized by that day and visibly shaken, Karina continued with her story:

"I was shocked because I didn't know where the house was. I didn't know where it was. I tried to ask people, and they said, 'Yes, this is Alabama.' I went up and down the street twice, and I didn't have a cell phone, and I didn't know where I was. The street was Alabama, it was just the different side of Alabama. Someone finally told me to try the other side. I had to cross Highway 6, and I was so scared, because cars go everywhere. But then I found the house, and then I got home, and I was crying. I was really scared. That was really bad, that I didn't know where I was and the bus driver was like, 'Why don't you just get off now'."

Karina emphasized that this event was scary for her, not just because she felt so helpless and confused, but because the driver was not understanding or sympathetic in any way. He forced her off the bus and left her alone in an unfamiliar neighborhood.

Food service personnel

Perhaps no part of our daily lives exemplifies our culture more than what we eat, and the cafeteria can be an extremely daunting and intimidating place for newcomers. For students who are unfamiliar with typical "American" food, the selection served in the school cafeteria could range from unfamiliar to completely bizarre. This unfamiliarity will be even more stressful if students have cultural or religious dietary restrictions to which they must adhere. Cafeteria workers should be sensitive to these concerns and take steps to alleviate this stress for newcomers. For example, students from some cultures may not eat beef, pork, or other meat products, such as gelatin (derived from the collagen of cows and pigs and found in gummy candies, marshmallows, gelatin desserts, and other dips and sauces). Additionally, some students may not combine certain foods, such as dairy and meat products, at the same meal.

For example, a group of Hindu newcomers at my school had an extremely difficult time navigating the lunch line. They were intimidated by the unfamiliar foods, and they were extremely reluctant to make a selection at the risk of eating something prohibited by their religious practice. The cafeteria worker, when insisting the students select at least one item, grew increasingly frustrated at their noncompliance. The confused students could not communicate with the cafeteria worker about their religious preferences, and the cafeteria worker could not understand why the students would not make a selection.

Cafeteria workers can help students by labeling certain foods with icons, such as a small picture of a pig or cow, or other pictures or keywords to help students identify the various foods being offered and their significant ingredients.

Custodial staff

Orienting all personnel who will interact with newcomers will help alleviate some of these culture clashes and help newcomers make a smoother transition into the routines of their new U.S. schools. Some secondary immigrant students may not be familiar with concepts that are second nature to us, such as the proper norms when using a public restroom. From my interviews with secondary newcomer ELLs, I learned of a custodian scolding a young lady for putting her toilet tissue in the trash can rather than flushing it down the toilet. The student was simply not accustomed to the plumbing in the United States and did not know she could flush the toilet tissue.

School secretary/receptionist

The school secretary or receptionist is often the very first person a newcomer and his family will interact with upon arrival at the new school. Although it's important for all families to receive a warm welcome, it is crucial for immigrant families. This first impression will set the tone and expectation for future interactions with school personnel, and that importance must be emphasized. Being aware that at any given time a family in which no one speaks or understands English may arrive at school to enroll a child and having a conversation about how to appropriately address that situation when it does occur are positive first steps in preparing for it. Encourage the school secretary or receptionist to be mindful of overall body language and facial expressions. A genuinely warm smile goes a long way to bridging a language gap, as do small gestures of kindness and patience. Consider the following scenarios:

Scenario A:

The high school receptionist sits behind a large desk in the front office. A family of four comes in to enroll their two daughters. With only a slight smile and a matter-of-fact, all-business tone, the receptionist says, "Welcome to XYZ High School. What can I help you with?" The parent begins to speak in a language the receptionist does not understand. The receptionist cuts the parent off mid-sentence, puts both her hands up with open palms, waves, and says, "Whoa, wait, I can't understand a thing you're saying. You'll need go sit over there (points toward the chairs lined up on the wall) and wait until I can get someone else out here to help you." Her slight smile has now been replaced with a scowl of impatience. The parents look at the direction the receptionist is pointing but seem confused as to what they're supposed to do. "Yes, go sit over there," the receptionist says louder, pointing more forcibly. The mother and father exchange a few words in their language and then go and sit down, still confused as to what they are supposed to do. The secretary takes a few more phone calls before she gets up from her desk to go get some help for the family.

Scenario B:

The high school receptionist sits behind a large desk in the front office. A family of four comes in to enroll their two daughters. With a warm and genuine smile, the receptionist enthusiastically says "Welcome to XYZ High School. What can I help you with?" The parent begins to speak in a language the receptionist does not understand. The receptionist continues to smile, listening intently, and waits for a natural break in the parent's speech. She then puts both of her hands out, palms up, and with genuine concern says, "I'm so sorry, I do not understand you. Would you mind taking a seat while I get someone to help you?" She comes out from behind her desk and, gesturing with both hands, leads the family toward the chairs lined up on the wall and offers them each a chair, motioning for them to sit. She then holds up one finger, saying, "One minute, please," and immediately goes to get help for the family. She continues to smile while feeling empathetic toward this family, imagining what it would be like trying to enroll her own daughter in school in a foreign country where no one understands her language.

Which school would you prefer?

Crossing guards

Traffic and pedestrian rules are by no means universal. In fact, traffic signals in some countries are more of a suggestion than an actual rule. Crossing guards should know that newcomers may not initially understand or follow the expected rules. For example, students coming from countries where traffic rules and signals are loosely followed may dart out across the street when no cars are coming instead of waiting until they are told to do so by the crossing guard. Crossing guards can be patient and calm when acclimating newcomers to the expected rules and procedures.

A teacher of newcomers at South Houston High School in Pasadena ISD brought a bilingual campus police officer to Parent Night to speak to her newcomer students and their parents about the importance of properly crossing the street. SHHS is located at the intersection of two very busy streets, and many newcomers live in the neighborhoods within walking distance from the school. Students were receiving tickets from campus police for not properly and safely crossing the street at the signal-controlled intersection, a very dangerous prospect on the busy streets surrounding the school. The teacher wanted to ensure that her newcomers understood the laws against jaywalking, both for their safety and to prevent any of them from getting citations.

Campus police officers and security

The biggest concern for campus police and security is the manner in which newcomers may perceive these individuals. Campus security and police officers should be aware that adults in official uniforms may be extremely intimidating to those students who have lived in countries with authoritarian rule, where police are corrupt and potentially quite dangerous. Campus police and security should consider introducing themselves to the newcomers in a friendly and nonthreatening manner, perhaps as part of the newcomer orientation process. They might consider visiting the newcomer classroom, where they can meet the students in a small, nonthreatening environment. The goal for this initial meeting is to establish rapport with the students such that, if any of the students ever needed to do so, they could seek out the assistance of either the police or campus security without any fear of danger or harsh treatment.

School psychologist

The school psychologist applies expertise in mental health to provide counseling, mentoring, and instructional services to help students academically, socially, behaviorally, and emotionally. The school psychologist may also partner with families, teachers, school administrators, and other professionals to create a safe, healthy, and supportive learning environment. School psychologists can offer therapeutic services to newcomers with mental, emotional, and behavioral difficulties that stem from their immigration experience. Newcomers experiencing culture shock, newcomers with possible PTSD (see p. 39), unaccompanied minors (see p. 41), refugee/asylees (see p. 37),, and any newcomer who may be feeling particularly overwhelmed could benefit from the services of the school psychologist.

School nurse

School nurses play an important and often overlooked role in the overall well-being of newcomers. Nurses have a unique opportunity to engage with students and their parents on vital health topics, so it is imperative that nurses be provided with basic information on the newcomers, such as country of origin, cultural facts, and native language. Nurses are also encouraged, more than any others, to use an adult interpreter to bridge language gaps. Students should not interpret for their parents or other students. Aside from privacy concerns, students may not have the knowledge or emotional maturity to serve as interpreters for medical and health concerns. Even the most basic health topics can be embarrassing, difficult to explain, or culturally taboo to discuss. If having an interpreter is not an option, nurses can learn or have available a few key words and phrases in the student's home language, such as "I can help you feel better" and "show me where it hurts." Nurses can also have posters, illustrations, pictures printed from websites, and other visuals to help with explanations of various topics.

These are some concerns school nurses may encounter with newcomers:
(Bureau of Refugees and Immigrant Assistance, n.d.; Whitman, Davis & Terry, 2010)

LACK OF INFORMATION OR EMPHASIS ON BASIC HYGIENE

Nurses may need to explain to some newcomers the hygiene expectations of the United States. This may be especially true for student refugees who have been living in refugee camps or other primitive conditions.

UNDIAGNOSED HEARING OR VISION PROBLEMS

In addition to testing for these problems, nurses can assist the newcomers and their families with obtaining glasses or hearing aids.

UNFAMILIARITY WITH WESTERN MEDICINE

Immigrant families may not understand the role of the school nurse. They may need an explanation of the school nurse's role and reassurance that the school nurse is authorized to help the student. Additionally, they may need reassurance that any medicine the nurse may dispense at school is safe for students, pending parent permission and any known allergies the student may have.

USE OF ALTERNATIVE AND TRADITIONAL MEDICINE

There are many cultural beliefs and practices surrounding health and healing. Immigrant families may be using herbal therapies, prayer, or elders in the community to treat illnesses that require more formal medical intervention. Also, some cultures rely heavily on superstitious beliefs and behaviors in lieu of formal medical treatment. Nurses should be aware of any prominent and common alternative treatments in newcomers' cultures.

OTHER UNDIAGNOSED CONDITIONS:

Lead poisoning
Post-traumatic stress disorder
Nutritional deficits
Learning disability
Food and other allergies from first-time exposure
Mental illness

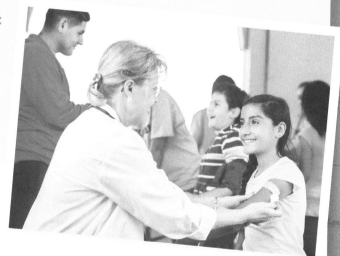

ELL Graduation Coach

An ELL Graduation Coach may have any of several different titles depending on the school or district. Some schools refer to this person as the Sheltered Instruction Peer Facilitator, and still others call this person the ELL Liaison. Regardless of the exact title, the role of ELL Graduation Coach is fairly similar from one location to the next. It is a multifaceted position with the overarching goal of improving the educational experience of ELLs. The ELL Graduation Coach supports the ELLs' social, emotional, behavioral, and academic well-being in preparation for graduation. This role may be part administrator, part counselor, part school psychologist, part social worker, and part interventionist, among others. Some responsibilities of the ELL Graduation Coach are:

- Consulting with ELLs to address academic, emotional, and social concerns

- Designing and implementing intervention programs to help ELLs get back on track/catch up

- Consulting with any other stakeholders regarding an ELL's behavior, academic achievement, or other important issues that pertain to his or her schooling

- Instructional coaching or modeling to assist teachers in designing lessons, improving the delivery of instruction, and increasing overall student achievement

- Working with teachers to utilize and embed technology into lessons and helping newcomers learn to use new technology

- Collaborating with administrators to address discipline and other issues

- Collaborating with counselors to review and analyze transcripts and create schedules

- Attending and often facilitating professional learning communities (PLC) or teaming time

- Building connections among home, school, and the community

- Planning and facilitating parent meetings, parent nights, and other parent events (Donuts with Dad, Muffins with Mom, etc.)

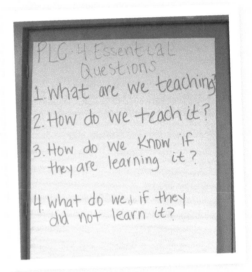

- Assisting in the evaluation of ELLs for special services or advanced classes

- Reviewing testing data

- Designing student progress monitoring systems

- Overseeing compliance to state and federal policy/participation in meetings related to ELL placement

- Designing, presenting, and helping sustain campus and district ELL staff development

- Improving the school climate for ELLs and promoting ELL inclusion through multicultural/cultural proficiency training

I know this list of stakeholders is quite lengthy, and you may be thinking that some of the scenarios and suggestions seem a little above and beyond. However, to say it "takes a village" to meet the cognitive, affective, and emotional needs of newcomers would be an understatement. I am reminded of an administrator I know who helped establish and supervise the newcomer center on her campus. Of the many things she did to help support newcomers on her campus, she had the district transportation office on speed dial. She frequently made calls and sent emails to district transportation, keeping the lines of communication open for discussion on such issues as bus routes, late buses for after-school tutoring, and transportation for students to and from school on Saturdays to accommodate field trips and more tutoring. She made sure the drivers knew who her newcomers were, where they lived, and what stops they needed to get off at. This constant flow of communication between the school and the transportation office helped alleviate the kind of problems Karina experienced in the previously mentioned scenario (see p. 63).

What could an effective teaming model to support newcomers in a school look like?

As a young teacher first being trained to meet the diverse needs of ELLs, I was one of a few teachers selected to be part of our school's sheltered instruction (SI) team. Everyone selected for the team was expected to identify with the dual role of being not only a content teacher, but also a language teacher. With the newly hired team in place, we were given a great deal of support and training to ensure our implementation of SI was effective in meeting the needs of our ELLs. We were also given a second teaming period, allowing us to meet daily with the sole purpose of discussing student achievement and addressing individual student needs.

Following a professional learning community model, meetings were highly organized with various roles for all participants and concise record keeping via agendas and minutes. We discussed issues such as grades, discipline, attendance, and overall achievement of the students. Additionally, we shared ideas on strategies, activities, lesson planning, and instructional delivery. If multiple members of the team had a concern with the same student, we had the ability (and were given the authority) to include that student in the

meeting so that he or she could be part of the discussion and solution. We also often included the student's grade-level assistant principal and/or counselor if the issue warranted a more serious intervention.

All the students assigned to our team, both ELLs (including newcomers) and non-ELLs, knew they were part of our team. The students knew they had the same core teachers, and they were aware that these discussions were taking place. They were quick to discover that their underachievement in one class might lead to a conversation with three additional teachers throughout the day. Conversely, we also celebrated students, and if a student met a goal or had some other success in a class, he or she would likely be congratulated for it throughout the day by other members of the team.

The teaming model also helped us to implement a very effective tutoring schedule. If all four of us teachers could not stay after school on one particular day, the students could go to another teacher on the team and get the extra help. Because we had so many students staying after school so regularly, we often served light refreshments so students could come, have a small snack, and get a little extra help and support. After-school time was also reserved for team parties in which students were welcomed and encouraged to come for a variety of celebrations, including student of the month, holidays, and other cultural celebrations.

With a solid teaming model in place, coupled with our highly effective multi-layer intervention process, we did not give students the opportunity to fail. That simply wasn't an option. There were many safety nets available that were put swiftly into action when a student showed signs of struggling. That's not to say that all students achieved at the same level. Of course, even with all of our support, we did not have 100 percent success. We did, however, have fewer failures, fewer students leaving school never to be heard from again, fewer disciplinary issues, and significantly more student success overall.

After the first year as a team, we noticed a phenomenon among the faculty. Many teachers who were initially quite reluctant to work with ELLs, who did not volunteer for the ELL team when they had the initial opportunity, began to inquire as to how they could get a spot on the team. Instead of the stigma of "more work" and "those kids," the SI team became the team to be on, and the ELLs became the kids everyone wanted to teach. This remains one of my proudest achievements as an educator of ELLs: helping others see these kids in the same light as I do, as amazing and hard-working students who just need to be given an opportunity to succeed with a little love and support.

The following year, as our ELL and newcomer ELL population grew, so did our team. As we added more teachers who were well-trained and who implemented SI strategies with fidelity, we continued to see student achievement increase, student dropout rate decrease, and graduation rates increase as we became even more skilled in meeting the needs of the ELL and newcomer ELL population.

To administrators:

I know it's not feasible for every school to offer teachers an extra conference, team time, or even the high level of training we received that initial year, but be creative and think out of the box with regard to teacher and resource allocation. Consider creating a team of master ELL/newcomer teachers. What incentives can you offer these teachers to make the extra work they will be doing, at least initially, enticing for them? Additionally, I know it is often the master schedule that dictates which teachers are assigned to what conference, planning periods, or teams. It is also common knowledge that the master scheduler must work around a number of complicated variables to make a master schedule work. However, not everyone has a heart for ELLs, and it is crucial for ELL success to match the right teachers with the right kids. Teaching newcomers is by no means an easy job. It takes blood, sweat, and tears (figuratively and literally!) and a heart of gold. It can be a frustrating and overwhelming, especially at first, when you have to teach difficult content concepts to a student who does not understand a single word of English. I know it takes a heart to teach all kids, but I think it takes a very special heart to teach newcomers. To the best of your ability, try to match those teachers who have that special heart with the newcomer population.

FABIO ADVISED THAT TEACHERS SHOULD MAKE AN EFFORT TO CHECK IN WITH THE NEWER

students and make sure they understand. He described for me his own experience: "I had the strength to go and tell them I'm a new student, and I'm learning English, but some of the other students don't do that, and teachers don't know that they need the extra help. If you know that they're new, that they're learning the language, just go ahead and ask them, 'Are you okay? Do you need anything?'"

Fabio continued: "The thing that teachers shouldn't do is make you feel like you don't belong here. Be a little patient. We will get it, but just be patient, and show us that you care, that we should do our part. Tell us, 'We're here for you, but if you need anything, just don't doubt letting us know.'"

ACTIVITY 7

Eyes on the Expert

Context:

Teacher/Teachers

Description:

The goal of Eyes on the Expert is for you as the teacher to grow in your understanding of how to work effectively with ELLs. Each teacher chooses another expert teacher of ELLs, and they plan, conduct, and reflect on a classroom observation together. Spending time watching another teacher who is skilled at working with ELLs is one of the most effective ways to improve one's own craft (Seidlitz, Base, Lara, & Smith, 2016).

Directions:

A: Identify the Expert

Talk to your colleagues, administrators, and ELL specialists at your campus and in your district to find out which teachers are highly effective at working with ELLs. Effectiveness with ELLs can include any of several achievements:

- Building rapport/relationships with ELLs
- Creating a positive classroom climate
- Creating a culturally responsive classroom
- Structuring conversations where ELLs participate
- Getting ELLs to read effectively
- Getting ELLs to write effectively
- Getting ELLs to meet content-area goals
- Teaching vocabulary to ELLs

B: Plan the Observation

1. Meet with the person you plan to observe, and discuss what you will be looking for in the observation. For ideas on focal points, see the form on the following page. Make sure that the person you are observing understands that you do not expect them to have a flawless lesson or classroom. You are simply looking for ideas that will improve your instruction by seeing how your colleague works with ELLs. Remind them that you have chosen them because their campus or district colleagues consider them to have expertise in working with ELLs.

2. Choose a time or class period that works best for you and the teacher being observed.

3. Find out if it is OK for you to talk with students and view sample work.

4. Plan a time after the observation to conduct a post-observation discussion.

C: Conduct the Observation

1. Find a place in the room where you can quietly observe the teacher and students interacting and working together.

2. Use a form like the one bleow to record observations, reflections, or questions you may have as you watch the expert in action.

D: Conduct Post-Observation Discussion

1. Meet with the teacher at the pre-planned time.

2. Share with them what you thought was most effective during the lesson, and thank them for their time and willingness to work with you.

3. Ask them what they thought was working best with ELLs during the observed lesson.

4. Ask them how they establish rapport with ELLs and go about creating a positive classroom climate.

Topics	I observed . . .	I am wondering . . .
Content and language objectives		
Vocabulary instruction		
Variety of techniques to make content comprehensible		
ELLs' reading and writing		
Student–student interaction		
Linguistic accommodations: Sentence stems, native language resources, word banks, low risk environment for language production, etc.		

ACTIVITY 8

Cardio Check-in

Context:
Teacher/Self, Teacher/Colleagues, Teachers/Campus

Description:
This survey helps teachers as individuals or as members of a teaching community to think through their current level of knowledge and concern about ELLs. The responses can serve as a basis for planning ways to focus attention on ELLs on campus (Seidlitz, Base, Lara, & Smith, 2016).

Directions:
1. Teachers meet together as a campus or team and fill out the Cardio Check-In survey individually.

2. Teachers discuss their answers in small groups of three or four colleagues. They then share their observations with their campus or team using the stem, "We noticed..."

3. Teachers then discuss their thoughts using the stem, "We need to..." in small groups and then share those thoughts with the campus or team. As a group, try to select the top two or three answers from the "We need to..." column. These can serve as the basis for action steps to be taken by the campus or team.

Rate yourself on a scale of 1 to 5 on how much you agree or disagree with the following. *(1 is strongly disagree, 5 is strongly agree. Circle one)*

1.	I want to know more about how I can better serve the ELLs on our campus.	1 2 3 4 5
2.	I know a lot about the background and experiences of the ELLs I teach.	1 2 3 4 5
3.	I think our campus effectively reaches out and connects with the parents of our ELLs.	1 2 3 4 5
4.	As a campus we provide enough academic support for our ELLs.	1 2 3 4 5
5.	As a campus we provide enough social support for our ELLs.	1 2 3 4 5
6.	I know effective ways to promote English language development in my classroom.	1 2 3 4 5
7.	I know how to help ELLs be successful in the classes I teach.	1 2 3 4 5
8.	I know which ELL program models are in place on our campus.	1 2 3 4 5
9.	I am familiar with the different languages and cultures of ELLs represented on our campus.	1 2 3 4 5
10.	We have a campus plan for welcoming new ELLs.	1 2 3 4 5

ACTIVITY 9

Let It Go

Context:

Teacher/Self, Teacher/Teachers

Description:

This activity helps us clarify what issues we have control over in working with learners and what issues are beyond our control. By clarifying this, we are better able to meet the needs of our students by narrowing our focus (Seidlitz, Base, Lara, & Smith, 2016).

Directions:

1. Have a meeting to discuss ways to improve instruction for ELLs.

2. Have everyone present individually respond to the stem, "One challenge facing ELLs is..."

3. Have everyone share his or her responses with a partner.

4. Create a two-column chart in a clearly visible place, and have everyone read off the challenges that ELLs are facing. The two columns are "Things we have control over" and "Things we don't have control over." As teachers share their challenges, each person must state into which column the particular challenge should be placed. Challenges that the campus has only partial control over will be placed in the center of the chart.

5. When all the challenges have been shared, erase all the challenges that the campus does not have any control over. Examples might include things such as state policies related to ELLs, the language used in the home, and the educational level of children when they arrive.

6. Rank each of the remaining challenges on a scale of one to five as to how effective teachers are as a campus in meeting those challenges.

   1: Not at all effective at meeting the challenge

   2: Not very effective at meeting the challenge

   3: Somewhat effective at meeting the challenge

   4: Effective at meeting the challenge

   5: Very effective at meeting the challenge

7. Discuss as a group how the campus can improve on meeting the challenges that are not yet being met effectively.

ACTIVITY 10
Four Things ELLs Must Hear

Context:

Teachers/Campus; Teacher/Students

Description:

Four Things ELLs Must Hear is an approach to meeting the affective needs of newcomers in order to generate a growth mindset toward success in learning language and content.

This activity involves the teacher planning concrete ways to communicate four specific messages to newcomers. These messages are communicated directly to the students, and they create a context for teachers' interaction with newcomers (Seidlitz, Base, Lara, & Smith, 2016).

FOUR THINGS ELLS MUST HEAR	
You are important.	
What we are learning is important.	
You can do it.	
We will not give up on you.	

Directions:

1. Create a chart with four columns that show the four messages you want to communicate to your newcomers:

   • You are important.

   • What we are learning is important.

   • You can do it.

   • We will not give up on you.

2. Fill out each column with a list of concrete ways that you can communicate that particular message to your newcomers. For example, in the first column, list specific ways you can help your newcomers realize that they are important members of the learning community. In the second column, list specific approaches to helping students realize that what they are learning is significant to them and to others. In the third column, list ways you can support students in realizing that they are capable of accomplishing their learning goals, and identify ways you can support students who are not feeling successful. In the last column, list ways to create opportunities for students to support one another in the classroom. This is particularly helpful for newcomers and other beginning-level students who are in heterogeneous classrooms.

3. Share your four-column chart with colleagues, and periodically review and reflect on your approaches to meeting the affective needs of your newcomers.

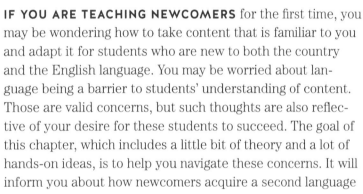

CHAPTER 3
CREATE COMPREHENSIBLE LESSONS

IF YOU ARE TEACHING NEWCOMERS for the first time, you may be wondering how to take content that is familiar to you and adapt it for students who are new to both the country and the English language. You may be worried about language being a barrier to students' understanding of content. Those are valid concerns, but such thoughts are also reflective of your desire for these students to succeed. The goal of this chapter, which includes a little bit of theory and a lot of hands-on ideas, is to help you navigate these concerns. It will inform you about how newcomers acquire a second language and why that knowledge will aid you in creating lessons that are comprehensible, interactive, and designed to ease the perceived burden of the language barrier.

Process of Second Language Acquisition

What is second language acquisition (SLA)?

The term *second language acquisition* refers to the process by which someone acquires a language during late childhood, adolescence, or adulthood after they have learned their first language (Ortega, 2009). The process of SLA differs from first language acquisition in that second language acquisition typically occurs in older learners. These learners often have a greater range of academic experiences and background knowledge to draw on, which may help them in acquiring literacy in a new language.

Why do I need to know about second language acquisition as a teacher of newcomers?

Did you take a foreign language in high school or college? Are you currently fluent in that language? For most of us, the answer is no. Why is that? How did most of us spend two or more years "learning" a language that we now, for the most part, cannot speak or understand? Part of the answer can be explained by Krashen's theory of second language acquisition (1981). Essential to Krashen's theory is the difference between learning a language and acquiring a language. He argues that one acquires a language through natural processes and cannot learn a language by memorizing vocabulary and grammar rules—the way that many of us were taught in our foreign language classes. Understanding Krashen's distinction between learning and acquiring a language is helpful when teaching newcomers. The following questions highlight this and other key aspects of his theory that are critical for teachers of newcomers (such as the affective filter, the silent period, and comprehensible input), along with their practical instructional and classroom implications.

What is the difference between "learning" a language and "acquiring" a language?

Language learning is the product of formal and systematic instruction in vocabulary and grammar. Language acquisition, even for a second language, is a subconscious process very similar to the process children undergo when they acquire their first language. Acquisition requires meaningful, authentic interaction in the target language, while learning is a conscious process resulting in knowledge of the language. One might learn such things as grammar, syntax, and form, for example. Learning the language is what we experienced in most of our formal language courses in high school and college, and acquisition is what begins to happen when you start "picking up" Spanish on your vacation to Mexico.

In the content-area classroom, teachers provide the opportunity for language acquisition rather than focusing on language learning. Language is acquired as students use it to fulfill authentic purposes like getting basic needs met and reading, writing, or talking about relevant classroom content with peers and the teacher. In a class where English language development is the focus, there is a balance between learning and acquiring English as students get practice with authentic language as well as direct instruction in English grammar, syntax, structure, and mechanics. We will discuss this further in Chapter 4.

What is the affective filter, and why is it significant?

The affective filter is the matrix of emotional and motivational factors that may interfere with language acquisition. This may include factors such as anxiety, self-consciousness, boredom, annoyance, alienation, lack of motivation, etc. These affective variables greatly influence students' abilities to acquire a second language. Low motivation, low self-esteem, and anxiety "raise" the affective filter and form a mental block that prevents ELLs from understanding words and phrases that enable language acquisition. This includes the words and phrases essential to understanding key content-area concepts. Simply put, when the filter is "up," language acquisition is impeded. One analogy that I have used to explain this concept comes from the idea of "shields" common in sci-fi movies. When the shields are up, nothing can get in or out. Conversely, when a language-learning environment is created that fosters high motivation, self-confidence, positive self-image, and a low level of anxiety for the learner, the affective filter is lowered; the shields are down.

How can I keep the affective filter low?

The following list contains ideas for maintaining a low affective filter for your newcomer ELLs:

- Create a welcoming learning environment in which ELLs feel secure

- Encourage a collaborative and noncompetitive (nonthreatening) environment where students receive consistent input and feedback from the teacher.

- Provide a motivating environment that lowers the students' anxiety, thus encouraging students to take risks with a new language.

- Honor the silent period, and do not force students to speak when they are not ready and willing to do so (see p. 80).

- Avoid overcorrecting. See the paragraph below for more information on error correction with newcomers.

What are best practices for error correction with newcomers?

ELL newcomers often express a strong desire to speak correctly in English. However, when they begin to take risks and speak in class for the first time, it must be in a low stress environment. Correct form and correct grammar are not the primary focus for teachers of newcomers. Rather, students should be encouraged to take risks and try the new language without fear of continuous error correction from the teacher or other students. One strategy helpful to content-area teachers is recasting. Teachers recast when they reword or rephrase a student's grammatically incorrect statement using correct grammar without forcing the student to repeat it correctly. For example:

Student: *"George Washington **goed** to Valley Forge."*

Teacher: *"That's right, Javier. George Washington **went** to Valley Forge."*

Of course, using professional judgment and considering such factors as the language level of the students, the context of language use, and the personal goals of each student, teachers can make individualized decisions as to how and when they will provide correction.

WHEN ASKED TO DESCRIBE HIS TEACHERS OVERALL,

Fabio described them as friendly. "I think the thing that kept us going is when you find people like that, friendly people that want you to learn and care about the things you're going through and stuff like that." I asked Fabio to elaborate on how he knew whether or not a teacher cared, and he launched into an enthusiastic description of his biology teacher:

"Yes! Oh my God. My biology teacher, he was a great person. He would encourage us every day. Every day. He talked to us every day about 'How are you doing? Are your parents coming to pick up your progress reports?' or 'How are they?' Every day. He was very awesome." Fabio said this was important because a more personal relationship with teachers made it easier for him and his fellow students to ask questions and seek help when needed.

What is the silent period, and why is it significant?

The silent period, also called the pre-production stage, is an interval of time during which newcomers do not independently communicate in English. This does not mean they are not learning. They can participate in activities such as copying text and repeating phrases. Newcomers need time to listen and observe, to process and internalize what they hear, and to develop receptive, and eventually expressive, vocabulary. Language skills are developing at this point, but speaking skills typically emerge significantly later than listening skills. Newcomers in the silent period should not be forced to speak if they are not ready. From the very beginning, newcomers are capable of learning new concepts and acquiring new language.

How long does the silent period last?

The silent period may last anywhere from a few days to a few months or more, depending on a variety of factors. The following factors may increase the length of the silent period:

- Student's Personality

  – Quiet, shy, introverted students tend to take longer before they feel comfortable speaking.

- Cultural Difference

  – In many cultures, for example, females are expected to remain quiet while males are encouraged to speak out.

- Quality of Instruction

  – A classroom that does not provide opportunities for authentic peer interaction and maintains a high affective filter will discourage verbal expression.

What are the stages of second language acquisition?

All new learners of English progress through the same stages to acquire language; however, the length of time each student spends at a particular stage may vary greatly. The following chart summarizes each stage:

TABLE 3.1 Stage of Language Acquisition

Stage (Average length of time in stage)	Description Students...
Pre-production (0 to 6 months)	• have up to 500 words in their receptive vocabulary; • are learning and acquiring language every day, but are not ready to speak (silent period); • can listen attentively and may be able to copy words from the board; • will be able to respond to pictures and other visuals; • can understand and duplicate gestures and movements to show comprehension; • benefit from the repetition of English; • may tire quickly and/or become overwhelmed after a short amount of time, as listening to and trying to make sense of the English language all day can be cognitively exhausting for newcomers; and • can repeat what they hear (parroting).
Early production (6 months to a year)	• will develop a receptive and expressive vocabulary of about 1000 words; • begin to combine words into short phrases and can use short language chunks that have been memorized during the silent period; and • will often use incorrect grammar.
Speech emergence (1–3 years)	• have a vocabulary of about 3,000 words; • can use simple sentences and phrases; • can ask simple questions and carry on short conversations; • will initiate short conversations with classmates; and • will occasionally use incorrect grammar.
Intermediate fluency (3–5 years)	• have a vocabulary of about 6,000 words; • will attempt to use more complex sentence structures and ask comprehension/clarification questions; and • can express opinions and share their thoughts.
Advanced fluency (5+ years)	• demonstrate grade-level performance in academics; • have mastered complex structures of the language and can apply these structures in speaking and writing; • have close to native fluency; and • will most likely exit from the ESL/ELD program.

Note. Different states have different ways of classifying the sequence of stages of language development. Several states use WIDA, in which the stages of language development are (from lowest to highest) Entering, Beginning, Developing, Expanding, Bridging, and Reaching. Several other states use ELPA21, in which the stages of language development are classified as Beginning, Early Intermediate, Intermediate, Early Advanced, and Advanced. Additionally, several states have developed their own standards. For example, in Texas, the stages of language development are classified as Beginner, Intermediate, Advanced, and Advanced High.

Teaching Content to Newcomers

What is comprehensible input?

Comprehensible input is one of the most important SLA concepts to understand when teaching content to newcomers. The term refers to any written or spoken messages that students understand in a second language because of the context. It is part of the language acquisition hypothesis first proposed by Stephen Krashen (Krashen, 1981). Imagine a teacher saying the following:

"Remember that, when converting a fraction to a decimal, you divide the numerator into the denominator."

If the teacher is pointing to an example of a fraction, a decimal, a numerator, and a denominator, the newcomer ELL will better understand what these terms mean and be able to acquire some English while listening to the teacher. However, if the teacher is not providing context clues (such as pointing to visuals), a newcomer ELL will not likely understand nor acquire any English while listening to the teacher. Lessons are comprehensible when the teacher implements strategies that effectively bridge the language gap for the students. For example, if a teacher provides information by simply lecturing to the class, the newcomer will not likely receive (understand) that input and thus will comprehend very little, if any at all, from the lecture. However, if that same teacher provides an outline of the notes, presents visuals that correspond to the information being presented, uses body language and gestures, and speaks more slowly, the newcomer is likely to get a great deal more out of the lecture. Essentially, comprehensible input strategies are anything a teacher does to help students understand the language while content is being presented, even when students are at a lower level of English language proficiency.

Why is providing comprehensible input the most critical skill for teachers of newcomers?

Newcomers often spend most, perhaps all, of their days being instructed in a language they do not understand. Because of this, it is critical for them to receive a high degree of comprehensible input, especially when they are responsible for gaining content knowledge as well as language. Without effective comprehensible input, students' instructional time is, in a word, wasted. Students may spend day after day attending a class, never really understanding what is going on, much less gaining any useful content knowledge.

LUCY EXPLAINED HOW MANY OF HER TEACHERS MADE AN EFFORT TO MAKE THEIR CONTENT more comprehensible to her and other English language learners. Lucy described teachers using pictures, body language, gestures, and simple language to describe and define major content concepts. Lucy gave the example, "Something easy, like if you didn't know what 'empty' meant, they'd just say, 'If you know what full means, it's the opposite.' That helped a lot."

When students do not receive effective instruction via purposeful, comprehensible input, no distinction can be made between content knowledge (or lack thereof) and limited English proficiency. Thus, any assessments or grades become obsolete. Without comprehensible input, there simply isn't any language development.

What are best practices for providing comprehensible input for newcomers?

There are two main ways that teachers increase the amount of comprehensible input they are providing for newcomers. The first is to ensure the students have opportunities to activate prior knowledge and build necessary background knowledge. The second is to provide contexts that enable the understanding of language. The following two charts represent key concepts, best practices, and strategies that teachers can use for each:

TABLE 3.2 Activating Prior Knowledge and Building Background

BEST PRACTICE	DESCRIPTION & DETAILS
Connecting Concepts to Students' Experiences	Choose examples of content concepts that are relevant to the personal, cultural, or world experiences of the newcomers: • Geography and biodiversity from home countries • Historical figures and events • Musical and artistic traditions • Literature, stories, and folktales Provide opportunities for students to share their experience and knowledge of content concepts.
Teaching Vocabulary	Focus on content-specific and non-content-specific academic vocabulary. NEWCOMER VOICES *Karina explained to me* that there were words she knew the concept of, but not the English word. "I had a lot of trouble with science, because there are a lot of words that I didn't know, like feedback. I remember that one because it was my first test and I didn't know what feedback meant. I didn't know what it meant and I felt so bad, because my test was like 50 something, and I wanted to cry because I was always an A student in Mexico, come here and I have like 60 something in my class. Then I asked Mr. Valdez what does feedback mean and he explained to me in Spanish. I was like, 'Oh, I know that! I know what that means! I know what that question is asking now.'" She stressed that knowing or understanding that one word would have made the difference for her on that exam. Have students create personal dictionaries or glossaries to keep a record of newly learned words. Have students write, draw, and create their own materials: • Books • Flashcards • Study guides Provide students with bilingual dictionaries and encourage (require) their daily use. Identify cognates with students as part of your daily routine. Explain the meaning of new words in context.

BEST PRACTICE	DESCRIPTION & DETAILS
Cooperative Learning Strategies	Allow brief, frequent opportunities for students to clarify their understanding within small groups. Use QSSSA (see p. 132) • Question: Teacher asks question • Signal: Students show readiness to respond with signal • Stem: Teacher provides sentence starter • Share: Students discuss responses with peer(s) • Assess: Teacher randomly selects students to respond Teach social and language skills: • Getting into groups • Taking turns • Encouraging one another • Providing peer feedback • Using sentence stems
Note-taking Tools	Use graphic organizers so students can visually see how concepts are related: • Semantic maps • Story maps • Venn diagrams • Flow maps • Timelines • Foldables™ NEWCOMER VOICES When asked for advice on classroom tools, Diego cited "worksheets" as something he really liked. He liked them because they broke the lesson into what he referred to as "sub-lessons," which he learned in chunks. Upon further questioning and elaboration, I realized that Diego was referring to various kinds of graphic organizers that his teachers often made use of in class. He gave a specific example from world geography in which pictures of the continents were accompanied by "little boxes where we wrote the information." Students were to write a summary of each of the continents after the graphic organizer was completed, and his teacher graded each one separately and provided immediate feedback. Chunk information into smaller, student-friendly pieces. Incorporate interactive notebooks.

TABLE 3.3 Providing Contexts that Enable Understanding of Language

BEST PRACTICE	DESCRIPTION & DETAILS
Using Visuals and Supplemental Materials	Create a print-rich environment that includes various elements: • Word walls • Anchor charts • Sentence stems • Other content visuals (maps, charts, signs, content posters) Add labels to posters and other classroom visuals. Convey critical information in a text through use of the visuals: • Steps of a process • Significant events • People • Key concepts Use visual representations of new vocabulary: • Graphs • Photographs • Drawings • Charts NEWCOMER VOICES Karina suggested that teachers use pictures and visuals along with bilingual glossaries to give meaning to lessons and vocabulary. She provided an amusing example and was adamant in her point: "If I see a picture of a goat, I know it's a goat. I may not know goat in English, but I know it's a goat. A goat is a goat. You see a picture of a goat in Korea, you see a picture of a goat in Africa, you know it's a goat. It's a different word, but it's still a goat." Use supplemental materials: • Video clips • Audio recordings • Computer programs • Children's books • Chants and music • Poetry
Adjusting Manner of Speech	Provide clear explanations for academic tasks: • Use clear, short sentences. • Model steps. • Refer to a visual. Use gestures strategically. Adjust your rate of speech. Use simple language structures. Limit idioms, colloquial phrases, and slang. Avoid adult sarcasm. Paraphrase to clarify words and phrases. Model correct language usage. Refer to demonstrations, models, and visuals when lecturing. Use repetition of sentence structures and sentence stems. Vary facial expressions and intonation appropriately.

BEST PRACTICE	DESCRIPTION & DETAILS
Checking for Understanding and Providing Feedback	**NEWCOMER VOICES** **Diego described to me how quizzes** were given each class period over that day's lesson. Mr. Baker gave these quizzes to ensure that students understood the material before moving onto something new the following day. Diego explained that these daily assessments were very beneficial. "I keep more stuff in my head and remember it better. The other teachers, they were pretty different. We would still go over stuff as a class, but they wouldn't give us that much quizzes. We would probably have maybe one or two quizzes, then we would just wait for the end of the six weeks for the next test." Diego emphasized that he liked that Mr. Baker checked for understanding along the way because then Diego always knew how he was doing in that course.

Avoid "yes/no" and generalized "Do you understand?" questions addressed to the whole class.

NEWCOMER VOICES

I asked Diego if he ever felt bad asking questions in class, and he explained that although he did not have an issue with seeking assistance from teachers, several of his classmates were not comfortable doing so. "They would rather ask me than ask the teacher, because they would feel that they were dumb, and they would ask me instead." Diego recommended that teachers not wait for immigrant students to seek help on their own. Rather, he suggested that teachers closely monitor these students and consistently check for understanding with direct, one-on-one questioning. Going further, he explained that general questions directed to the whole class, such as "Does everyone understand?" are not effective, because he and other students would likely just say "yes" or nod their heads in agreement. Diego claimed that checking for understanding with individual students was the only effective way to ensure that everyone was being helped and supported. Furthermore, he advised that "teachers should be very understanding with the students so they can feel more sure of themselves, asking questions rather than just staying quiet and missing some important things you might need to know."

Increase your wait time to allow students the extra processing time to

- consider the question,
- formulate an answer, and
- find the words they need in English.

NEWCOMER VOICES

I asked Lucy if she had any advice or recommendations for teachers. Lucy immediately replied, "Patience." When asked to elaborate why, she explained, "Because I could be that kind of girl that learns fast, but there are so many students that [don't], so you have to be patient and try to explain things easier, in a better way." Lucy also recommended that teachers "use lots of pictures, repeat things, and not talk too fast" so ESL students can understand the concepts.

BEST PRACTICE	DESCRIPTION & DETAILS
Utilizing Movement	Use paired language and movement to elicit physcial response (TPR) from the students and to check for understanding (Asher, 1969).

"Please hold up your books." Hold up your own book to model.

"Show me with your hands, on a scale of one to three, how well you understand." Hold out your own hand and demonstrate.

Use physical activities when possible:

- Hands-on experiences
- Manipulatives
- Interactive lessons

Have students act out content information, for example:

- Roles in a food web or food chain
- Historical narrative
- Plot to a story or a plot diagram
- Number lines
- Students as parts of a classroom-sized graphic organizer (Venn diagram, timeline, etc.)

Adapting Content-Area Texts

Record texts for students to listen to, with clearly enunciated speech:

- Summaries of lectures and notes
- Excerpts from textbooks
- Parts of fictional text

Highlight and annotate texts and provide copies

Chunk text into smaller, more manageable sections

Rewrite sections of text in simplified English (see p. 107-109)

Help ELLs become acquainted with their textbooks (table of contents, glossary, index, etc.)

What is sheltered instruction, and what does it look like in a content-area class with newcomers?

Sheltered instruction (SI) is an approach to teaching ELLs that utilizes a variety of strategies and best practices to provide meaningful instruction in the content areas (social studies, math, science) regardless of the ELLs' language proficiency. Effective sheltered instruction teachers typically have a working knowledge of second language acquisition processes, and they integrate language as well as content instruction into daily lessons. Whereas language is the primary focus in an ESL class, content is the focus in an SI content class.

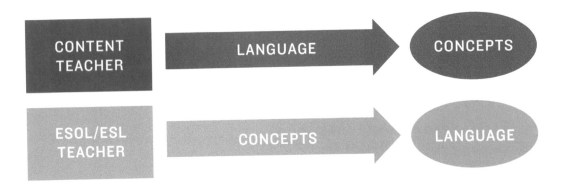

Sheltered instruction refers to grade-level instruction where teachers use special techniques to make the lessons comprehensible to ELLs. "The word 'sheltered' is a metaphor for simplifying the language without watering down the content" (Wright, 2010, p. 84). When sheltered instruction began, students were often separated from the mainstream population into classes consisting solely of other ELLs, and they were not expected to compete academically with native English-speaking students. This is no longer the case. Although some classes may now consist solely of ELLs, this is often only the case with newcomer classes (see scheduling, p. 157). The majority of ELLs beyond their first or second year in U.S. schools are grouped with their English-speaking peers. Additionally, all ELLs, regardless of their time in U.S. schools and with few exceptions, are held accountable for the same curriculum and content standards, take the same high-stakes assessments, and are required to meet the same standards for graduation. Thus, the term "sheltered instruction" is now generally understood as a set of best practices and effective strategies teachers use as a pathway to grade-level content mastery and English language acquisition.

In a sheltered instruction classroom where newcomers are present, it is critical that the teacher use **targeted comprehensible input along with second language acquisition strategies** to teach content. "Best practice for second language learners requires that teachers do whatever is necessary to make the content accessible and comprehensible while providing students the opportunity to interact with, connect to, act on, talk about, read about, and write about important ideas and information. To teach on the second language pathway is not to dumb down or reduce expectations or teach what is easy" (Commins, 2012, p. 46).

What is the distinction between social and academic language?

Jim Cummins (1979, 1981) first highlighted the distinction between social and academic English with regard to the timelines and challenges that ELLs encounter as they attempt to catch up to their fluent, English-speaking peers. Basic Interpersonal Communication Skills (BICS), also known as conversational fluency or social language skills, are the "surface" skills of listening and speaking that are typically acquired quickly as students interact with native speakers. Cognitive Academic Language Proficiency (CALP), also called academic language proficiency or academic language skills, include the ability to understand and express, orally and in writing, grade-appropriate academic language relevant to success in school. Cummins argues that many newcomers develop conversational fluency (social language/BICS) within two years of immersion in the target language, but that it takes between five and seven years for a newcomer become proficient in academic English (CALP) at the same level as native speakers. The following chart summarizes some key differences between social language and academic language

TABLE 3.4 Characteristics of Social and Academic Lanaguge

Social Language Basic Interpersonal Communication Skills (BICS)	Academic Language Cognitive Academic Language Proficiency (CALP)
• 0–2 years to develop	• 5–7 years to develop at the level of native speakers
• Many opportunities to seek clarification	• More difficult to clarify
• Simpler language (shorter sentences and simpler vocabulary and grammar)	• Complex language (longer sentences, technical vocabulary, and more complex grammar)
• Usually simpler, more familiar topics (movies, friends, daily life)	• Complex topics, often abstract, cognitively complex
• Usually face-to-face, small number of people, informal settings	• Lecture-style/textbook communication, little situational context
• Precise understanding is seldom required	• Precise understanding and description or explanation is required; higher-order thinking
• Many clues available to help with meaning (expressions, gestures, social context)	• Fewer clues available to make meaning; students often have less background knowledge on which to build

Why is the distinction between academic and social language important to me as a teacher of newcomers?

It is likely that newcomers will have a working grasp of social English within a short period of time after beginning school in the United States. By the end of their second year, those students will likely have a high degree of conversational fluency. However, educators should not assume that ELLs who have attained a high degree of fluency and accuracy in everyday, spoken, social English have corresponding proficiency in academic language. Problems arise when educators assume or think that a student who demonstrates good social English is proficient in academic English. Mistaking BICS for CALP can lead to very unfortunate results for the newcomer, such as referrals for special education services when all the newcomer needs is more time and practice in the target language.

What are linguistic accommodations?

Linguistic accommodations are specific supports that teachers of ELLs can use to modify their instruction to help ELLs understand content and acquire academic language. **Such accommodations also enable ELLs to receive comprehensible input with low-stress opportunities to produce output (i.e., talk and write).** They include things such as planning for student–student interaction, adjusting one's rate of speech to match a student's proficiency level, and providing visuals and gestures during instruction. Adapted text and supplemental materials are two more examples of linguistic accommodations.

What are some linguistic accommodations specific for newcomers?

The following chart represents some effective accommodations for newcomers at the pre-production, early production, and intermediate stages of language proficiency.

TABLE 3.5 Possible Accomodations for Newcomers

Listening *Teachers...*	Speaking *Teachers...*	Reading *Teachers...*	Writing *Teachers...*
Allow use of same language peer native language support	Provide short sentence stems and single words for practice before conversations	Organize reading into chunks	Allow drawing and use of native language to express concepts
Expect student to struggle to understand simple conversations	Allow some nonparticipation in simple conversations	Use visual and linguistic supports	Allow students to use high-frequency, recently memorized, and short, simple sentences
Use gestures and movement	Provide word bank of key vocabulary	Explain classroom environmental print	
Provide visuals, slower speech, verbal cues, and simplified language	Model pronunciation of social and academic vocabulary	Use adapted text	Provide short, simple sentence stems with present tense and high-frequency vocabulary
Pre-teach vocabulary before discussions and lectures	Allow extra processing time	Allow wide range of reading	Allow writing on familiar, concrete topics
Teach phrases for student to request that speakers repeat, slow down, or rephrase speech	Provide sentence stems with simple sentence structures and tenses	Allow grade-level comprehension and analysis of tasks including drawing and use of native language and peer collaboration	Avoid assessment of language errors in content-area writing
	Model and provide practice in pronunciation of academic terms	Provide high level of visual and linguistic supports with adapted text and pre-taught vocabulary	Provide simple sentence stems and scaffolded writing assignments

Planning Sheltered Instruction Lessons for Newcomers

How do I plan a sheltered instruction lesson with effective comprehensible input for newcomers?

Beginning with your state's curriculum, identify the specific objectives of what you're expected to teach. You should have a clear and concise objective for each section of the curriculum you plan to teach.

- Example: "Students will **explain reasons for the involvement of Texas in the Civil War.**"

- Non-example: "Students will learn about the Civil War."

In the example above, the difference is the focus on specific content that the student will have to understand and explain, per the state curricular standards. Such specificity provides a more effective path for the teacher to plan a targeted lesson that teaches content while building language. It also allows the teacher to determine what language, concepts, and vocabulary need to be pre-taught or provided to the newcomers.

In planning a comprehensible lesson for newcomers, ask yourself the following questions:

- How will I link the content to the newcomers' culture and prior knowledge, and how will I build background information? (videos, images, books, etc.)

- What key terms will I post to my word wall/word bank, and what images can I use to represent the words?

- What do I need to prepare as a teaching aid (maps, charts, flash cards, graphic organizers, outlines, etc.) before teaching the lesson?

- How will I use visuals, movement, and cooperative learning in the lesson?

- Do I need to adapt any text? If so, how? (see pp. 107-109)

- What methods of home language support will I use? (see p. 102)

What do I need to provide newcomers with before I deliver a lesson?

It is often helpful to provide newcomers with information at least one day before a lesson is delivered. Providing students with this information ahead of time gives them an opportunity to begin processing. Newcomers can use translation devices to translate the information into their home language or go over it with another student, a tutor, or a parent. Ideally, before the teacher even begins the unit or the lesson, students have a firm grasp of what will be taught.

The following pages provide for an example of the information that might be provided to newcomers prior to a unit on cells.

*TAKE NOTE

Consider providing students with the following before a lesson:

- A list of the key vocabulary students are expected to know

- An adapted or modified version of the text

- A native-language summary of the information

- Links to online resources that can provide background information

INTRODUCTION TO CELLS: BASIC STRUCTURE AND FUNCTION

OBJECTIVES:

Identify the main ideas of the cell theory
Compare and contrast prokaryotic cells and eukaryotic cells
Identify the structure and function of the parts of a eukaryotic cell
Compare and contrast the structures of plant and animal cells

VOCABULARY REVIEW:

Organization – the orderly structure of cells in an organism
Enzyme – a protein that speeds up the rate of a chemical reaction

VOCABULARY:

Cell	Cytoplasm
Cell theory	Endoplasmic reticulum
Organelle	Golgi body (apparatus)
Prokaryote	Vacuole
Eukaryote	Lysosome
Nucleus	Chloroplast
Plasma (cell) membrane	Chlorophyll
Cell wall	Mitochondria
Nucleolus	Cilia
Ribosome	Flagella

--UNIT OUTLINE--

I. The Discovery of Cells
A. The cell theory
1. All organisms are composed of one or more cells.
2. The cell is the basic unit of structure and organization of organisms.
3. All cells come from other, preexisting cells.

B. Two basic cell types
1. Prokaryotes
a. Cells that do not contain any membrane-bound organelles
i. Bacteria
2. Eukaryotes
b. Cells that contain membrane-bound organelles
i. Protists, fungi, plants, and animals

II. Eukaryotic Cell Structure
A. Cellular boundaries
1. Cell wall
2. Cell membrane

B. Cell control
1. Nucleus

C. Assembly, transport, and storage of materials
1. Nucleolus
2. Ribosomes
3. Cytoplasm
4. Endoplasmic reticulum
5. Golgi body
6. Vacuoles
7. Lysosomes

D. Energy transformers
1. Chloroplast
a. Chlorophyll
2. Mitochondria

E. Locomotion
1. Cilia
2. Flagella

F. Division
1. Centrioles

How can I arrange my classroom to support newcomers during a lesson?

To support newcomers during a lesson, have student seating arranged to encourage opportunities for frequent peer interactions in partners or small groups. In addition, consider establishing a regular procedure for recording your lesson so newcomers can access it outside of class. In sheltered settings, teachers often support content and language acquisition by posting the following:

- Content and language objectives
- Sentence stems
- Key vocabulary on a word wall/word bank
- Agenda outlining the day's tasks

How do I ensure newcomers receive comprehensible input during a lesson?

The most important factor in ensuring ELLs receive comprehensible input during lesson delivery is to continuously check for understanding throughout the lesson. This can be accomplished by observing how students respond to instruction and questions. Teachers can also use techniques such as quick-writes and active response signals.

When students are not able to comprehend the language, teachers can increase the use of visuals, realia, and gestures to emphasize and clarify meaning and allow students to see the words as they are spoken (see Point and Talk, p. 118). In addition, teachers can reduce the amount of "teacher talk" and simplify their directions (see SIP, p. 117). Teachers might also want to consider using shorter, simpler sentences and more common vocabulary when newcomers are struggling with comprehension. Self-reflection can also be helpful. Teachers can ask themselves, "If this lesson were in Danish, Hungarian, or some other language, would I understand?" For other suggestions on increasing comprehensible input, see the "Best Practices" charts on pp. 83-87.

How can I deliver my lesson in such a way that newcomers gradually become more independent learners?

One way to help newcomers become more independent learners is to explicitly teach learning strategies. Learning strategies are processes students use to help themselves "comprehend, learn, or retain new information" (O'Malley & Chamot, 1990). Some examples of ways teachers can help newcomers develop learning strategies are the following:

- Teach students to categorize their information using graphic organizers
- Demonstrate highlighting techniques
- Model your thinking processes for students using "think-alouds"
- Teach ELLs to find definitions for key vocabulary in the text

How do I ensure newcomers understand content concepts during a lesson?

Teachers often struggle with ways to ensure that newcomers in their classrooms are understanding key content concepts during a lesson. There are two ways teachers can ensure newcomers understand key concepts. The first is to deliver instruction in such a way that newcomers are more likely to understand the concepts. The second is to continuously check for understanding throughout the lesson. The following chart gives examples of both.

TABLE 3.6 Newcomers' Understanding

Increasing Newcomers' Understanding	Checking Newcomers' Understanding
Consistently connect new concepts to newcomers' prior knowledge and cultures	Have students use total response signals (see p. XXX)
Use concrete, real examples	Have students demonstrate understanding on paper (writing, drawing, creating an example, solving, etc.)
Allow opportunities for home language support	Monitor conversation during student–student interaction
Explicitly reference visuals (pointing, drawing, etc)	Ask questions using common English vocabulary and simple sentence structures
Provide frequent opportunities for interaction	

What are some ways I can reinforce newcomers' learning after a lesson?

There are a variety of ways teachers can reinforce learning for newcomers, including:

- Making copies for newcomers of the notes fluent English speakers, or students at higher levels of English proficiency, took during the lesson
- Providing videos (with closed-captioning if possible) or audio recordings related to current lesson concepts
- Giving newcomers follow-up activities that reinforce vocabulary and concepts
- Having students review the lesson in small groups or pairs
- Adjusting homework assignments to your newcomers' English language proficiencies

What are some challenges for newcomers in specific content areas?

Whether you are the content-area or ESL teacher, it is important to be mindful of the challenges facing newcomers within specific content-area classes (Haynes and Zacarian, 2010). This is crucial so that you can effectively help your newcomers not only comprehend the content material, but acquire academic English as well.

TABLE 3.7 Newcomers and Content

Content Area	Challenges	Content-Specific Accommodations
Reading	Frequent use of figurative language, idioms, imagery, and symbolism in text	Use of vocabulary scanning
	Prevalence of vocabulary not commonly used in social English	Discuss with students context of literary work before reading
	Understanding connotation and denotation of words	Provide bilingual/monolingual dictionaries of English idioms
	Technical literary terms (plot, climax, stanza, alliteration, etc.)	Provide story summaries, outlines
	Lack of experience in analyzing literature	Choose literature that also exists in the newcomers' home language
	Variety of text structures found in literature	Explain varied grammatical conventions found in different genres (use of vernacular, flexible punctuation, etc.)
	Presence of English-language dialects within literature	Outline differences in structure among various genres
	Unfamiliarity with common themes and genres	
	Presence in literature of deviations from standard grammar	

Content Area	Challenges	Content-Specific Accommodations
Mathematics	Difference in linguistic formation of numbers Use of decimal point versus comma Difference in algorithms for problem solving Standard System versus Metric System Difference in cultures' timings of when topics are taught (i.e., estimating, rounding, and geometry are taught early on in U.S. schools) Lack of familiarity with style of word problems common in the United States. Difficulty of translating mathematical terms Mental math versus "shown" math in work and assessments	Explicitly identify and explain U.S. math conventions (decimal points, commas, spoken versus written numbers, etc.) Provide explicit instruction/tutoring in Standard Measurement system Present word problems as a genre of writing (common words, phrases, structures, etc.) Allow flexibility in problem-solving methods, if students can demonstrate success Provide resources in newcomers' home language for use outside of class
Science	Vastness of science-specific vocabulary, including new meanings for previously known, simple words Complex, multi-step directions in labs Prevalence of multiple new concepts within single page of science text Complexity and abstractness of visuals Complex sentence structure and passive voice used in textbooks	Teach prefixes, suffixes, and roots Use SIP (see p.117) Always have visuals and checklists for multi-step processes Create a "Pay Attention To" list that directs students toward what to focus on in a text Simplify visuals, and present them in context Provide outlines and adapted texts
Social Studies	Lack of prior knowledge of U.S. history, government, geography, current events, Western political ideas, and related vocabulary Prominence of figurative speech (synecdoche, metonymy, hyperbole, etc.) in text Use of passive voice within social studies text Prominence of lecture/note-taking method of instruction Presence of visuals not directly related to topics within textbooks Difficulty identifying significant people, events, and concepts within a text	Provide resources on unfamiliar social studies topics in newcomers' home languages Supplement lecture with videos (preferably with closed-captioning) for students to watch outside of class Highlight and explain examples of figurative speech in text Consistently reference visuals during lectures Intersperse lectures with brief opportunities for clarification via student–student interaction Have students frequently use total response signals (see p. 119) during lecture to express understanding

Cooperative Learning

Why is cooperative learning so effective for newcomers?

Cooperative learning is effective for all types of students because it promotes learning and fosters respect and cooperation among diverse groups of students. Students learn to depend on each other in a positive way to accomplish a variety of learning tasks. Cooperative learning is especially beneficial to newcomers because it not only helps the development of language, but it also helps the learning of content concepts in a structured, safe, and nonthreatening way. Cooperative learning encourages cooperation rather than competition. The latter is often the norm in a traditional, teacher-centered classroom where students "compete" with other students to answer questions, for opportunities to speak, and for the teacher's attention. In cooperative groups, newcomers also get the opportunity to observe how their peers (both same-language and native-English speakers) learn and solve problems while the newcomers learn to express themselves with greater confidence and in a more natural context.

What are some best practices to ensure cooperative learning is effective?

In addition to the above best practices, Kagan (2009) uses the acronym PIES to explain the four principles of cooperative learning that, when in place, produce the most effective results.

Positive Interdependence

Individual Accountability

Equal Interaction

Simultaneous Interaction

Positive Interdependence

You have positive interdependence when there is a positive correlation between outcomes; a gain for one student is a benefit for another. Students work together in a group to accomplish a common goal. If students feel they are on the same side and are not competing with each other, they are more likely to work together, encourage, and assist each other. Likewise, groups must be given tasks where each person's contribution is necessary—tasks that require working together.

Individual Accountability

Although teams work together to accomplish a goal, individual students are ultimately responsible for their own performance. See the section on assessments and grading (p. 106) for ideas on how to appropriately and authentically assess newcomers.

Equal Interaction and Simultaneous Interaction

Participation is highly correlated with achievement (i.e., mastering a new skill requires practice). However, participation is often lower among ELLs, especially newcomers, who often lack the language and confidence to participate at the same level as more advanced ELLs or native English speakers.

Simultaneous interaction actively engages a majority of students at once. For example, in a traditional classroom, a teacher may ask a question, that only one student (usually the one who volunteers) gets to answer. In simultaneous interaction the teacher may ask a question then have everyone turn and tell a partner the answer. In the latter example, all students have the chance to think about and share their answer. This is especially critical for newcomers because they will greatly benefit from the increased wait time and opportunity to discuss their response with a peer.

To encourage equal and simultaneous interaction, keep groups small. The ideal number is no more than four students per group, with an occasional group of three or five depending on the number of students in your class. Smaller groups encourage active participation by all members of the group, and groups of four can easily split into pairs when needed. Next, provide structure within the group so that each student is encouraged and has the opportunity to participate. Without structure, newcomers may take a more passive role in the group, making the cooperative opportunity ineffective for them. Also, consider establishing procedures, protocols, and expectations for such things as staying on task, assisting each other, encouraging each other, agreeing and disagreeing with each other, and giving and receiving feedback from peers. Provide sentence stems so students have access to the language needed to accomplish these expectations.

How should I group my newcomers for cooperative learning?

There are a number of grouping configurations when it comes to newcomers. They can be grouped with other newcomers, with other ELLs at different language proficiency levels, or with a combination of ELLs and native English speakers. Each grouping configuration provides different linguistic and academic benefits, and one is not necessarily better or worse than another. **How newcomers are grouped depends on the instructional goal you have for the lesson or part of the lesson, and the configuration may change frequently.**

Newcomers who are grouped with native English speakers benefit from listening to and interacting with the native speakers. However, being with only native speakers may be stressful and overwhelming for the newcomers, especially when they are in the pre-production or early production stage of language acquisition (see p. 81) and communication is still so difficult.

Conversely, grouping newcomers with only other newcomers, especially if they share the same L1, does not provide the opportunity to engage in authentic conversation with English-speaking peers, and the L1 may be the primary (and sometimes only) language used in the group. A homogeneous group of newcomers works best for small-group instruction when a teacher can work with the group to reteach or clarify an academic concept.

The third option, newcomers with other ELLs and with native English speakers, is typically where most newcomers will spend the majority of their time. This configuration provides the newcomers the benefit of working with other students with the same or similar language needs, allows for peer support in the L1 (if there are students in class with the same L1), and provides newcomers the opportunity to interact with native English speakers.

NEWCOMER VOICES

HETEROGENOUS GROUPING

Jesús described how he also received a great deal of support and strength from his fellow classmates, both other ESL students as well as non-ESL students, many of whom were bilingual. Although Jesús attended his English class with only other English language learners, his mainstream courses, math, science, and social studies, were attended by both ESL students as well as non-ESL students. Jesús explained that having students in class who spoke both English and Spanish was beneficial to him, especially in his first year, when his English proficiency was so limited:

"You go to your class in English, learn the language, then you go to your regular math, your regular social studies, your regular science class with [a] mix so there are other students there that really know the language [English], but some speak Spanish, a couple of students from your group. That really helps me because it gave me that confidence that, if I didn't know something in English, I could say it in Spanish and somebody is able to help me."

COOPERATIVE GROUPING/HOMOGENEOUS GROUPING (WHAT NOT TO DO)

One challenge for Karina was the isolation she often felt as an ESL student. She mentioned that some teachers would isolate the ESL students into one group when the class had cooperative learning tasks to complete. Karina assumed it was the teachers' way of helping the students, but to Karina and her fellow ESL students, it had the opposite effect.

She was adamant that this was something teachers should avoid. "Even though we seem like we're working, do not leave us alone." When I asked for clarification, she explained, "We do a lot of teamwork, but it's bad to leave only the Spanish speakers doing it and only the English in another group because whatever we don't know, we don't know." Karina elaborated that putting only immigrant, Spanish-speaking students in a group by themselves not only made them feel singled out but was also ineffective because there were no English-speaking students to use as a resource. She illustrated that in homogenous groups of only immigrant students only about "30 percent" of the work got done because of the language barrier. If the group didn't have enough English proficiency to complete a problem or task on the given assignment, they "would just skip it." As Karina advised, "Don't segregate the Spanish speakers, because we do feel it. Even though you're trying to help us, I didn't like it. Why are you leaving me with all the Mexicans in our little corner? I'm still a person, and I don't like feeling special."

First Language (L1)/Home Language Support

What are some appropriate ways to use a newcomer's home language to support instruction if the teacher speaks the same language?

When using the home language, teachers need to remember that their goal is to increase the total amount of English comprehensible input. In sheltered classes, English is the main language for instruction. However, using a student's home language can lower the affective filter and make the student feel more comfortable and welcomed. It is also serves as a time-efficient method of conveying meaning. The home language can be used to provide necessary background, help students understand directions, and clarify key concepts. The key thing to remember is that the home language is used to clarify key concepts and is not the main vehicle for instruction. Newcomers in content-area classes need both content and English language development. With these considerations in mind, the following is a list of appropriate ways for a teacher who knows a newcomer's home language to use that language to support instruction:

- Helping a student feel welcome
- Communicating with parents
- Communicating to newcomers that their culture and background are celebrated
- Maintaining rapport

In what ways can peers that speak the home language of the newcomer provide support?

The judicious use of a newcomer's home language with same-language peers can be beneficial when it comes to discussing and processing information and asking questions. Clarification of key concepts by other bilingual students can be quite helpful when other methods of explaining a word or concept have been exhausted (i.e., comprehensible input strategies and linguistic accommodations). It is not helpful to expect students to continuously translate lessons for the newcomers—neither for the newcomer nor for the students translating. Instead, use the same-language peers initially when the student is acclimating to the school, but avoid excessively relying on them for assistance. Meanwhile, scaffold lessons sufficiently so the newcomer can move away from using the peers once his or her own language development is increasing.

How do I support newcomers in their home language when no one in the class speaks that language?

When neither the teacher nor any students in the classroom speak the same language as a newcomer, there are still ways to use the newcomer's home language as support. Upon arrival, the teacher can find a list of common cognates (if any) that may be present in the newcomer's home language. As mentioned above, direct translation of the content from the teacher may not be feasible, and the newcomer could benefit from the use of an electronic translator or bilingual dictionary and/or glossary.

When multiple languages are present in the classroom, the teacher can create multilingual word walls by using a bilingual dictionary or Google Translate for creating a list of key vocabulary in multiple languages. Google Translate's phone app can not only translate words typed in directly, but also translate words viewed through a smartphone's camera. Newcomers can use this app to translate environmental print, such as posters, word walls, objectives, and anchor charts. Also, newcomers can use Google Chrome to translate entire pages on the web into a variety of languages. This way, teachers can assign web pages for newcomers to read related to topics that will be discussed in class.

What complications should I be aware of when providing home language support?

There are some complications that may arise when providing home language support to newcomers. Students may rely on translation at the expense of constructing meaning through context (e.g. teacher's comprehensible input: visuals, gestures, etc.), possibly slowing their English language development (Thornbury, 2010). Also, translation is sometimes not feasible in classes of mixed nationalities or where the teacher does not speak the learners' home languages. In such a situation, seeing the teacher provide assistance to other students may make a newcomer feel alienated and frustrated when he or she does not receive the same assistance.

WHEN I ASKED JESÚS WHAT HIS TEACHERS DID TO HELP HIM OVERCOME

the language barrier he experienced as a new student, he described being allowed to speak Spanish as a significant benefit. "They let us speak Spanish because they know it's hard. They understand the reasons why we were [speaking Spanish]. We were helping each other. They let us explain to each other. We also had the dictionaries and sometimes the aides would translate. And they were open to learn, too."

Jesús explained that he and his fellow ESL students would also teach the teachers basic words in Spanish while the students were learning English. "We helped them to learn a couple of words, and they helped us to learn the whole language," Jesús said. "They gave us the knowledge in their language, but still allowed us to talk about it in our language so we could understand it. They were patient enough to let us learn the language in our [own] time. That was something that helped us a lot."

Assessing Newcomers

How can I appropriately assess newcomers?

This is one of the most frequently asked questions I receive with regard to newcomers. Effectively and fairly assessing students on content knowledge when they have little to no English proficiency can be quite challenging. First and foremost, every effort must be made to assess content knowledge rather than language ability. For this, authentic assessments are a much more effective option for evaluating student achievement and attainment of content knowledge compared to a more traditional, paper-and-pencil, multiple-choice test. During authentic assessments students are expected to apply their skills to authentic tasks, projects, and activities. Additionally, one of the most effective ways to assess newcomers with limited English proficiency is to build assessment into instruction and, whenever possible, offer a variety of authentic assessments on a regular basis to measure achievement. The following chart includes examples of types of authentic assessments.

TABLE 3.8 Assessing Newcomers

The teacher creates/uses...	The newcomer creates/uses...
Rubrics	Drawings
Checklists	Response signals
Anecdotal records	Graphic organizers
Observational records	Audio or video recordings
Records/notes from teacher–student interactions	Timelines
Observations of student–student interactions	Learning logs
Peer or teacher evaluations	Reflection journals
Progress portfolios	Projects
Matching exercises	KWL charts
	Student projects
	Self-evaluations

How do I balance the requirements of standardized testing with authentic assessments?

Although it can take several years for immigrant ELLs to make academic gains equal to those of their native English-speaking peers, newcomers are still required to participate in standardized testing as outlined by federal and state accountability standards. To prepare for standardized testing, many schools and districts collect data through common curriculum-based assessments and exams (CBAs/CBEs), benchmarks, and even unit tests. When and to what degree newcomers participate in these assessments is up to the individual school or district. In some cases, newcomers take these tests with similar linguistic accommodations that would be offered to them on state assessments. In other cases, no linguistic accommodations are provided to collect baseline data. When teachers are trying to balance the requirements of standardized testing with the need to authentically assess newcomers, all these factors must be considered.

If linguistic accommodations are allowed for ELLs on curriculum-based assessments and/or benchmarks, it is helpful for teachers to consistently provide these accommodations for newcomers during instruction. For example, on some mandated assessments, ELLs are allowed to use dictionaries as an assessment. In this case, informing ELLs that dictionaries are an allowed accommodation, and providing classroom practice using a dictionary, is essential. This why it is important for content-area teachers to be familiar with the accommodations allowed for ELLs on mandated assessments.

Unfortunately, sometimes accommodations are not allowed on mandated assessments. In this situation, it is best for teachers to familiarize newcomers with the format of the assessment and help them to view the assessment as an initial step in their learning process. Of course, best practices would be to avoid having CBA/CBE or benchmarks "count" if newcomers have not been accommodated. Giving the test without accommodation is not effective because newcomers do not have sufficient English language development to be accurately assessed on content knowledge. However, if, due to situations beyond the teacher's control and best intentions, the test must count—as part of a grade or toward graduation—at a district or state level, teachers can explain to newcomers that they will measurably improve on these assessments as they acquire more English. Anecdotes can be helpful here. Teachers can invite former newcomers who have been successful on the assessment to share their experiences with current newcomers.

What are some linguistic accommodations I can provide during a traditional paper-and-pencil assessment?

When giving a more traditional paper-and-pencil assessment, a good rule of thumb to consider is:

If you provided accommodations for the content, then you should also provide accommodations for the assessment.

Some possible accommodations:

- Use of dictionaries or glossaries: standard English, ESL, or bilingual
- Extra visuals, pictures, or diagrams
- Lists of non-content-specific words (given ahead of time)
- Clear study guide in simplified English
- Extended time to complete assessment
- Taking assessment in small/quiet environment with one-on-one assistance

How do I grade my newcomers?

The purpose of grading is to provide information on how well students have mastered the learning objectives or goals established in a particular class. By using authentic assessments (see p. 104), teachers can more accurately record how well newcomers have mastered an objective. The more newcomers have demonstrated mastery of the learning objectives, the higher their grades should be. This will be the case even if their assessments are not identical to those of their English-speaking, or more proficient peers. Both the number and types of grades may vary, but all grades should reflect the extent of the student's content mastery.

When newcomers are not able to "get good grades," teachers can reflect on the amount of comprehensible input and the kinds of linguistic accommodations they are providing during instruction as well as on the assessments. A suggested best practice would be to continuously refer to newcomers' needs for linguistic accommodations and use the linguistic accommodations chart (p. 96) or other district-provided materials for suggestions when creating lessons, assignments, and assessments for newcomers.

ACTIVITY 11
Adapting a Text

Context:

Teacher/Self

Directions:

- Begin with an alternate text
- Eliminate adjectives and adverbs
- Eliminate clauses and/or shorten complex sentences
- Eliminate unnecessary sentences
- Change synonyms

OPTIONS FOR ADAPTING A TEXT

Example from Chaucer's *Canterbury Tales: The Prologue*

Begin with an alternate text

You may begin with a version of the text that has already been simplified:

- An abridged version
- Spark Notes or Cliffs Notes
- A graphic novel

The narrator opens the General Prologue with a description of the return of spring. He describes the April rains, the burgeoning flowers and leaves, and the chirping birds. Around this time of year, the narrator says, people begin to feel the desire to go on a pilgrimage. Many devout English pilgrims set off to visit shrines in distant holy lands. Many more choose to travel to Canterbury to visit the relics of Saint Thomas Becket in Canterbury Cathedral, where they thank the martyr for having helped them when they were in need. The narrator tells us that as he prepared to go on such a pilgrimage, staying at a tavern in Southwark called the Tabard Inn, a great company of twenty-nine travelers entered. The travelers were a diverse group who, like the narrator, were on their way to Canterbury. They happily agreed to let him join them. That night, the group slept at the Tabard, and woke up early the next morning to set off on their journey. Before continuing the tale, the narrator declares his intent to list and describe each of the members of the group. Source: Sparknotes.com

Eliminate adjectives and adverbs

He describes the April rains, the burgeoning flowers and leaves, and the chirping birds.

The narrator describes the rain, the flowers and leaves, and the birds.

Eliminate clauses and/or shorten complex sentences

Many more choose to travel to Canterbury to visit the relics of Saint Thomas Becket in Canterbury Cathedral, where they thank the martyr for having helped them when they were in need.

Many pilgrims choose to travel to Canterbury Cathedral.

The narrator tells us that as he prepared to go on such a pilgrimage, staying at a tavern in Southwark called the Tabard Inn, a great company of twenty-nine travelers entered.

The narrator explains that, while he was getting ready to go on a pilgrimage, he was staying in a town called Southwark at the Tabard Inn. While he was there, a large group of 29 travelers came in.

Eliminate unnecessary sentences

Many devout English pilgrims set off to visit shrines in distant holy lands.

Deleted

That night, the group slept at the Tabard, and woke up early the next morning to set off on their journey.

Deleted

Change synonyms

The narrator opens the General Prologue with a description of the return of spring.

> The narrator begins the General Prologue by describing spring.

Around this time of year, the narrator says, people begin to feel the desire to go on a pilgrimage.

> During spring, people feel like going on a pilgrimage.

The narrator opens the General Prologue with a description of spring. The narrator describes the rain, the flowers, leaves, and birds. During spring, people feel like going on a pilgrimage. Many pilgrims choose to travel to Canterbury Cathedral. The narrator explains that, while he was getting ready to go on a pilgrimage to Canterbury Cathedral, he was staying in a town called Southwark at the Tabard Inn. While he was there, a large group of 29 travelers came in. There were many different kinds of people in the group, and they were all going to Canterbury Cathedral also. The group said the narrator could go with them. Before continuing the story, the narrator says he will describe each member in the group.

Example from *Romeo and Juliet*

Original Version	Adapted Version
Prologue: In the streets of Verona another brawl breaks out between the servants of the feuding noble families of Capulet and Montague. Benvolio, a Montague, tries to stop the fighting, but is himself embroiled when the rash Capulet, Tybalt, arrives on the scene. After citizens outraged by the constant violence beat back the warring factions, Prince Escalus, the ruler of Verona, attempts to prevent any further conflicts between the families by decreeing death for any individual who disturbs the peace in the future. Romeo, the son of Montague, runs into his cousin Benvolio, who had earlier seen Romeo moping in a grove of sycamores. After some prodding by Benvolio, Romeo confides that he is in love with Rosaline, a woman who does not return his affections. Benvolio counsels him to forget this woman and find another, more beautiful one, but Romeo remains despondent. Source: Sparknotes.com	**Plot Overview:** In the streets of Verona (a city in Italy) a fight breaks out. This is another fight between the servants of two families. The two families are the Capulet family and the Montague family. Both families have a high social status. Both families have been fighting for a long time. A guy named Benvolio tries to stop the fight. Benvolio is a member of the Montague family. Benvolio gets involved in the fight when a guy named Tybalt arrives. Tybalt is a member the Capulet family. The citizens of the town are very angry because the two families keep fighting. The citizens of the town stop the fight. Prince Escalus, the ruler of Verona, arrives. Prince Escalus says anyone who fights again will be executed (put to death). Romeo, the son of Montague, meets his cousin Benvolio on the street. Earlier Romeo was very sad and was walking around a group of sycamore trees. Benvolio asks Romeo several times why he is sad. Romeo tells Benvolio why he is sad. Romeo is sad because he is in love with a girl named Rosaline. Rosaline does not love Romeo back. Benvolio tells Romeo to find another woman who is more beautiful. This does not help Romeo. Romeo is still sad.

ACTIVITY 12
Word Walls and Environmental Print

Context:

Teacher/Students, Student/Students

Description:

In classrooms with newcomers, the walls should "talk." Word walls and other environmental print are important scaffolds that help make the curriculum more accessible. A word wall is a list of key terms or a word bank of the most important content vocabulary. The best word walls are not static. Instead, they change throughout the year. New words are added, and words that have been mastered are deleted. An effective word wall becomes a silent teacher. It is always there to remind students of the vocabulary words in their lessons, to show the correct spelling of new vocabulary words, and to provide illustrations of the words. We make the most of the word wall when we refer to it often in our lessons and when students use the words many times in written exercises and in classroom conversation.

Directions:

1. Determine which words to post.

- For content word walls, select the 15–20 content vocabulary words (also known as brick words) most crucial to the current unit of study. Additionally, you might consider a scholarly word wall where you can post important process, function, and transition words (also known as mortar words) such as *represents*, *similar*, and *differentiate* and any other non-content-specific academic terms. Print out or hand-write the words on large index cards, sentence strips, or standard paper. The words need to be large enough to be seen from anywhere in the room (Helpful hint: You can create a PowerPoint presentation for each word wall and type one word per slide. When you print, select "Full page slides/one slide per page" and you'll end up with one word per 8.5 x 11 sheet of paper. You can also add pictures to the PowerPoint slides.)

- Where applicable, attach a visual to the word to provide additional support for students. Be mindful that for some abstract words a picture may be more confusing than helpful. For example, a picture of a mitochondria could most definitely be used for that vocabulary word; however, what picture would go with the word globalization? A picture of the earth might make sense to someone who already knows the word globalization, but this may be confusing to a newcomer. Consider introducing abstract words and their meanings before adding a picture.

- Change the word wall often. Remove mortar words that have been mastered and switch out brick words for each unit.

2. Organize the word walls.

- Words can be grouped alphabetically or categorized based on content concepts.
- Other possibilities: high-frequency words, frequently misspelled words, transition words and phrases, "words we use all year," and "words you've seen before (in past units)."

3. Use the words on the word walls.

- Do a daily "Word Walk 'n Talk." Select a handful of words from one of the lists to analyze, explore, and use in context. Challenge your students to use these words appropriately in sentences, and continually provide students with contextualized examples of academic terms.
- Play "Guess the Word." Give clues to a posted word and have students try to guess it. Your clues can be related to the following: number of syllables, parts of speech, sounds in the word, word within the word (morphemes), related words, definitions, descriptions, or sentence completions.
- Refer to the word wall words during lessons and in conversation.
- Encourage students to use the words in whole class and student-to-student conversations.
- Praise students when you catch them using the words.
- Require the use of specific words by including them in sentence stems or specifying a number of words to be used for student conversations and during writing tasks.
- Have students keep a personal version of the word walls in their notebooks/personal dictionaries.
- Ask students to look for the words in printed sources outside the classroom (e.g., newspapers, magazines, or books). This shows a real-world connection to the vocabulary studied in class.

Note: The goal is for all students to be able to read any posted words from their seats. Some teachers' best efforts at creating word walls have been sabotaged by the glare of lights on laminated words, words written at distracting angles, words posted on dark paper or printed in strange fonts, or words that are just too small. As you post words, sit in various desks and look around to make sure that you can read all the words on your walls.

Making the Most Out of Other Environmental Print

Enhance Your Posters

Attach language to any posted visuals or content posters in your classroom. A visual with few or no labels is nice, but not as powerful as one with the key words attached. Be sure students can read the words from their seats. Write the words using large print in an attention-grabbing color, style, shape, etc.

Create Anchor Charts

Anchor charts are content visuals (think large chart paper) created by the teacher (or students) that highlight really important parts of a unit or lesson. They help students anchor their thinking and remind students of the most crucial information presented to them. In elementary classes, anchor charts are usually made during the lesson, with the students. However, since most secondary teachers teach the same lesson multiple times a day, the anchor charts can be made ahead of time, used throughout the day, and posted for review later in the unit, semester, or year. Like word walls, teachers can refer to the anchor charts during lessons and have students use the anchor charts to check their work, validate their points, and as a reference during class discussions and writing tasks. The difference between anchor charts and notes the teacher may write on a whiteboard or present in a PowerPoint is that the anchor charts will remain posted and visible as a reference to students and as an instructional tool for the teacher after the lesson is over.

Student-created Visuals

Another effective way to give students additional exposure to new words is to have them draw the visuals. Provide a stack of blank 5 x 7 index cards and let students earn extra credit for creating visuals of your posted vocabulary. Select the best ones and post them right next to the words.

What if I don't have any space for a word walls and anchor charts?

Since environmental print is so crucial for newcomers, teachers may need to make some adjustments regarding what is posted on walls and around the classroom. Decorations that serve no instructional purpose may have to be replaced with content visuals such as word walls and anchor charts (see Clear the Clutter, p. 114).

Regarding word walls, since they are just lists of words, there are many options for where they can fit. A bulletin board or empty wall is an ideal location, but here are some alternative ideas:

- on the windows
- on the front of the teacher's desk
- on the side of the filing cabinet
- on closet doors
- above the whiteboard

Another option is to create a movable word list:

- Post words on a tri-fold board (think science fair).
- Place a cardboard box on top of a plastic turntable. Each side can represent a different word list that can be rotated as needed.
- Use large sheets of cardstock attached to coat hangers that can be displayed in the classroom when needed.

ACTIVITY 13

CI Resource Roundup

Context:

Teacher/Self; Teacher/Teachers

Description:

In this activity, teachers investigate independently or meet in teams to discuss what print resources are available to help newcomers gain more comprehensible input in content-area classes (Seidlitz, Base, Lara, & Smith, 2016).

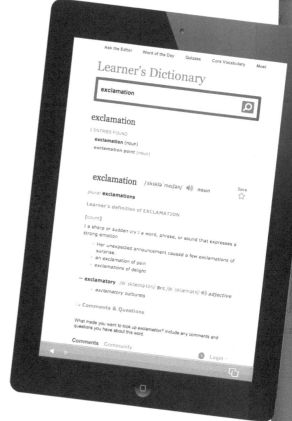

Directions:

1. Meet with a team of ELL teachers to discuss what specific resources are available for students to receive more comprehensible input during instruction. Resources might include things such as follows:

   - Adapted text
   - Simplified text
   - Translated text
   - Native language glossaries
   - Native language textbooks
   - Native language-related resources
   - Native language chapter summaries
   - Electronic dictionaries
   - Translated environmental print

2. Identify what resources you need to gather and provide for students.

3. Provide the materials to the students and explain how to most effectively use these resources to increase their comprehensible input during instruction.

   - It is better for students to read native language textbooks and related texts *outside* of class *before* the lesson in order to receive more comprehensible input during the lesson.
   - It is better for students to look at a *few targeted words or phrases* in an electronic dictionary rather than translating sentences or paragraphs.

ACTIVITY 14

Clear the Clutter

Context:

Teacher/Self

Description:

Research tells us that the classroom environment plays a very important role in effective instruction (Concordia University, 2017; Klein, 2016; Linsin, 2011). A well-organized, visually stimulating environment will enhance students' understanding of academic content whereas a disorganized, unkempt, or clutter-filled classroom can be distracting and confusing to newcomers.

Characteristics of a dapper, spruced-up classroom:

It's inviting

Students enjoy and appreciate walking into a bright, neatly arranged classroom. An organized, attractive classroom invites students in and makes them eager to be a part of what's happening inside.

It's calming

A clutter-free classroom will have a powerful effect on you and your students. A messy, unorganized room conveys a message of chaos and uncertainty while a clean, neat room has a calming effect.

It's a statement of respect

A well-organized room sends a message of respect—respect for learning, respect for your students, and respect for property.

It sets a tone

A fresh, appealing room environment that is tidy and well organized establishes a tone of professionalism, high expectations, and excellence. Students know you take pride in your work and your environment, and they are expected to do the same.

Take time for some honest self-reflection and really think about who and what the classroom space is for. **If your classroom looks like a yard sale or a teacher supply room, or it looks like it's been scooped up, shaken, and poured back out, it might be time to make some changes.**

Directions:

1. Apply a basic home decluttering strategy: If you have not used something in the last year, then you probably do not need to keep it. Additionally, if an item does not directly impact student learning, toss it, give it away, or store it someplace else.

2. Rethink the amount of personal "stuff" you have taking up classroom space. Your teacher desk and a few personal items, mementos, pictures, and such are perfectly acceptable, but rethink the shrine to your alma mater that is taking up a full bookshelf and adjacent wall. Students are the primary users of the space, and the environment should reflect that.

3. Revamp your wall space by removing old student work that is fading and curling. Rotate anchor charts, word walls, and other environmental print accordingly so walls do not get overly cluttered. Consider taking down other items that serve only as decoration and have no direct impact on instruction. The "Hang in There, Kitty" precariously hanging from a branch, Garfield "Learning by Osmosis" with the books strapped to his head, or the lone rower on the placid mountain lake representing "achievement" are all cute (albeit scientifically inaccurate in the case of Garfield), but they serve no purpose other than decorating your walls. With wall real estate at a premium, you must be very selective as to what you choose to post on your walls, and you should prioritize items that directly relate to content and/or language development.

4. Take inventory of other items around your room, where those items are, and whether they can be tossed or put elsewhere.
   - A messy teacher desk with papers piled up and various materials and resources here and there can be remedied by putting things away and recycling old worksheets and such.
   - Store cardboard boxes out of sight in another location or a cabinet instead of stacking them on counters or cabinets or in the corner.
   - Clean out disorganized and overflowing cabinets by recycling old paperwork and worksheets. Consider scanning papers and creating electronic copies so the paper versions can be eliminated.

5. After the clutter is gone, consider bringing in some elements of "home" to create what is referred to as the "Living Room Effect" (Concordia University, 2017). Items such as plants (real or artificial), lamps, rugs, a comfortable reading space, and perhaps even some inexpensive curtains or fabric to soften the windows will all help students feel welcomed, valued, safe, and secure.

ACTIVITY 15
CI Check-In

Context:
Teacher/Students

Description:
Teachers often struggle with finding ways to assess how well they are delivering comprehensible input to their newcomers. In this activity, the teacher asks newcomers to provide specific feedback on current teacher practices related to comprehensible input. "CI Check-In" facilitates meaningful interactions between students and teachers about instructional practices that impact learning (Seidlitz, Base, Lara, & Smith, 2016).

Directions:
1. Explain the concept of comprehensible input to your ELLs and include the following key ideas:
   - Comprehensible input happens when a student hears or reads a message that they can understand in a language they are learning.
   - When students hear a teacher speaking in a language and they understand the message, they are receiving comprehensible input.
   - When students read a text in a language they are learning and they understand it, they are receiving comprehensible input.

2. Explain to students why you want to increase comprehensible input in their instruction.

3. Provide the Comprehensible Input Survey to students and ask them to read each statement and rate it on a scale of one to five (one being "Never" and five being "All the Time"). If possible, have students write responses using sentence stems from the list below. You may need to translate this document into the home language of your students.

4. Discuss the survey results with your students and try to increase instructional practices that they have identified as helpful in providing comprehensible input. You should regularly check in with your students to see if the changes are working.

CI Check-In Survey

I understand the directions the teacher gives during class.	1 2 3 4 5
I understand directions better when _____.	
I understand when the teacher explains things in class.	1 2 3 4 5
When the teacher is explaining things, it would help if _____.	
I understand written directions.	1 2 3 4 5
I understand written directions better when _____.	
I understand what I am asked to read in class.	1 2 3 4 5
I understand what I read in class better if _____.	

ACTIVITY 16

SIP Directions

Context:

Teacher/Teacher, Teacher/Students

Description:

SIP is an acronym meaning "Short, Imperative, Pause" that teachers can remember in order to give clearer and more comprehensible directions to newcomers. Using SIP will result in streamlined directions that are easier for students to follow (Seidlitz, Base, Lara, & Smith, 2016).

Directions:

1. Memorize SIP to remember key ideas for giving directions to newcomers.
   - S=Short. Directions given to newcomers should always be brief and should avoid extraneous information not immediately necessary for the task. Sometimes it is important to "chunk" multi-step directions so that each step is manageable for newcomers to comprehend.
   - I=Imperative. Directions given to newcomers should be in the polite command form in English.
   - P= Pause. Teachers should pause after each short command. After pausing, teachers model the action the students are to perform.

2. Practice giving directions using SIP in front of a colleague, and ask for his or her feedback.

3. Increase the effectiveness of your instructions to newcomers by incorporating SIP.

Non-example:

"OK, class, we've been working on identifying the different parts of the cell and all the different functions of the various parts of the cell. What I want everybody to do now is take out your notebooks and flip them over to the last page we were working on. If you don't have your notebooks, that's OK, just go ahead and take out a piece of paper. I just want to see what you remember from yesterday's lesson. So please list for me every organelle you can remember, and next to it write down whatever you can think of related to the function of that particular organelle."

Example:

"Please take out your notebooks." Teacher holds up a notebook. "Open up to the next blank page." Teacher flips notebook to a blank page. "Think about what we talked about yesterday. Show me thumbs-up when you can remember some of the organelles we talked about yesterday." Teacher models the direction and waits until all students demonstrate that they remember some of the organelles. "When I say 'go,' write down all the organelles you can remember." Teacher walks around and assists any students who are struggling. "Now, next to each of those organelles, write down any of the functions you remember." Teacher walks around and assists any students who are struggling.

ACTIVITY 17
Point and Talk

Context:

Teacher/Self, Teacher/Students

Description:

Point and Talk is a means of providing comprehensible input while explaining content and giving instructions to newcomers. This strategy involves teachers intentionally developing the habit of using gestures to reference posted language, visuals, and resources while giving directions to students and discussing content (Seidlitz, Base, Lara, & Smith, 2016).

Directions:

1. Preview a lesson to identify which directions you must give to students orally and what key content concepts will be discussed.

2. Plan what objects you will hold, refer to, or use as models for the students while giving directions or covering key content.

3. While giving directions and explaining content, make eye contact with newcomers and occasionally use response signals (for example, "Rate yourself on a scale of one to five with your hand showing how well you comprehend") to measure students' understanding of the content and directions.

ACTIVITY 18
Total Response Signals

Context:

Teacher/Student, Student/Students

Description:

Total Response Signals are a way for teachers to enable students to self-assess and refocus during classroom instruction. Through this method, students can instantly show their current level of understanding or their thoughts on a particular issue or question without impeding the flow of instruction. This activity is particularly effective when working with newcomers who are in the pre-production phase (see p. 80) of language acquisition and are not quite comfortable with verbal output (Seidlitz & Perryman, 2011).

Directions:

1. Ask the students a question.

2. Tell all the students to show you a nonverbal signal that will indicate the choice they have made. (See chart at right.)

3. Make sure all students have indicated a response. This is the most significant step of Total Response Signals and is the reason why it is called a total response signal. The strategy is targeted toward ELLs, especially newcomers and other struggling students. Responding to the students when only high achievers have answered defeats the purpose of a total response signal.

4. After all students have indicated their response, have students share their thoughts with one another. Provide sentence stems to scaffold the language.

5. Once students are more comfortable speaking, you might consider adding a last step in which you randomly select a student to share his or her thoughts with the whole class.

Category	Signal
Written Response	Hold Up Paper
	Whiteboards
	Personal Chalkboards
	Answers on Cards
Ready Response	Hands Up When Ready
	Hands Down When Ready
	Thinker's Chin (hand off chin when ready)
	Stand When You Are Ready
	Sit When You Are Ready
	Put Your Pen on Your Paper When Ready
	Put Your Pen Down When You Are Finished
	All Eyes on Teacher
	Heads Down
Making Choices	Open Hand/Closed Hand
	Thumbs Up/Thumbs Down
	Pens Up/Pens Down
	Number Wheels
	Green Card/Red Card
	Move to the Corner/Spot You Agree/Disagree With Letter or Number Card Choices on a Metal Ring (A, B, C, D or 1, 2, 3, 4)
Ranking	Rank with Your Fingers
	Rank with Your Arm (the higher, the better)
	Line Up According to Response
	Knocking/Clapping/Cheering

ACTIVITY 19

Conversation Structures

Context:

Student/Students, Teacher/Students

Description:

Classroom management can be a concern when you have 25 or more students working in groups. Sometimes it borders on chaotic, but with a little bit of planning, teachers can structure student interactions so the interactions are controlled, productive, and fun. The ideas listed on this page give students multiple opportunities to interact with each other in an organized way to discuss the academic concepts of each day's lesson.

Directions:

Lines of Communication

Students form two lines facing one another. The students in each row share ideas, review concepts, or ask one another questions. After the first discussion, one row moves, and the other row remains stationary so that each student now has a new partner (Echevarria, Vogt, & Short, 2017).

Gallery Walk

Questions, prompts, or tasks to be completed are posted in various stations around the room. Students are assigned to a group. Each group is assigned to a station and given a specified time to answer the question or complete the task at the station. Groups rotate around the room until each group has visited every station (Santa, Havens, & Valdes, 2004).

Think, Pair, Share

The teacher asks a question and then provides wait time. Each student formulates an answer and then shares the answer with a partner. Afterward, selected students share their thoughts with the whole class (Lyman, 1981).

Inside/Outside Circle

Students form two concentric circles facing one another: an inside circle and an outside circle. Students then participate in a short, guided discussion or review with their partner. After the discussion, the outside circle rotates to the right while the inside circle remains still. All students now have a new partner for discussion (Kagan, 2009).

Clock Buddies

This is a quick and easy way to get students into pairs. Each student is given a clock face with blanks at each hour. Students make appointments with each other and pair up accordingly anytime during the lesson when students need to work in pairs.

For example: "Get with your 5:00 appointment, and come up with at least three reasons why the colonists revolted against the British during the American Revolution."

Round Robin

The teacher presents a category for discussion. Working in groups, students take turns naming, discussing, or characterizing ideas that fit in that category.

Roundtable

Present a category (e.g., names of body systems). Have students take turns writing one idea at a time.

Team Jigsaw

Each student on a team is assigned a piece of a text to read or a part of a topic to investigate. Students complete their sections independently then come back together as a group and share their sections or help assemble a team product by contributing a piece of the "puzzle."

Alternative: Expert/Home Groups

As students work on their assigned section, they can work with others in the class who have that same section. This is their expert group. After they have become experts on their piece, they return to their home groups to report out. Each home group should have an expert on each of the pieces.

ACTIVITY 20

List Group Label

Context:

Teacher/Students, Student/Students

Description:

In this activity, students organize vocabulary in a variety of ways to gain a deeper understanding of academic terms (Taba, 1967). List Group Label helps students understand the relationships between academic concepts and the meaning of academic terms. It is important for teachers to remember to provide students with sufficient background knowledge in order for students to participate in List Group Label.

Directions:

1. Give students a list of words, or have students brainstorm a list of words related to a given academic topic (they can even use the words from the word wall).

2. Ask students to copy the words or terms onto index cards or sticky notes, with one word per card/sticky note. Students can complete this step in groups.

3. Have students discuss the words and categorize them into piles based on similarities. Each pile must have at least two cards.

4. Have students create a label for each pile that explains how the words within that pile are similar. Students might label by topic, by part of speech, by characteristic, etc.

5. Have students compare their labels to see how other groups organize the same information.

Example: After finishing a unit on functions in math, the teacher and students might generate the following list:

range	expression	formula	parabolas
value	variable	quadrants	f(x) circles
equality	graph	input	ordered pairs
output	continuous	domain	polynomial
inequality	x and y	lines	vertical line test

After discussing and sorting the terms into groups, students might create the following labels:

Shapes	Representing functions	Included in a function
Parts of a function	Types of functions	

ACTIVITY 21
Concept Definition Map

Context:
Teacher/Students

Description:
Concept mapping helps students in two different ways. First, students can study a new word in depth. Second, concept mapping helps students define and describe unfamiliar words. To complete a concept map, students use a graphic organizer to identify the category and class, properties, or examples of the concept or target word.

Directions:

1. Distribute or have students draw a copy of the Concept Definition Map shown to the right (Moon, Hoffman, Novak, & Cañas, 2011).

2. Provide a target word or concept for students to insert in the center circle.

3. Have students work in groups of three to identify the category and properties on the concept map (What is it? What's it like?, etc.).

4. Ask students to write some comparison terms in the left circle.

5. Have students work individually on three illustrations for the last question: What are some examples?

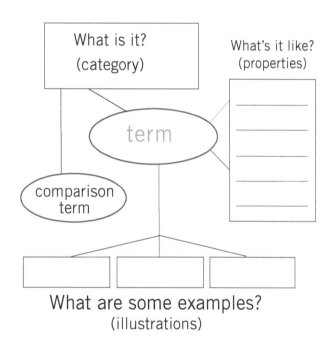

EXTENSION ACTIVITY Have students focus on the column in the Concept Definition Map titled "What's It Like?" Ask students to list words that describe the term in the center circle.

ACTIVITY 22

Describe, Describe, Draw

Context:

Student/Self

Description:

This is a simple, three-step strategy that teachers can use to build vocabulary in content-area classes. It gives students multiple exposures to new academic vocabulary and allows them to learn from their peers as well as their teachers.

Directions:

1. Describe a vocabulary word or term to students.

   - Select vocabulary words or terms that are content-focused and/or significant keywords in a lesson or unit (Marzano, 2004).

   - Access prior knowledge using visuals and student-friendly language to make sure students have an understanding of the vocabulary word or term.

2. Have students describe the term in pairs or groups.

   - Have students use their understanding of the teacher's description to describe the vocabulary word or term in their own words. Students can work individually or in groups to complete this activity.

   - Tell students that descriptions do not have to be complete.

   - Survey student work to make sure descriptions accurately reflect the meaning of the vocabulary word or term.

   - Have student groups complete the descriptions and share them with the class. Ask students to add information they learn from other groups to their notes.

3. Have students draw a representation of the vocabulary word or term.

   - Ask students to create a drawing that represents the meaning of the vocabulary word or term using icons, stick figures, or symbols to illustrate key ideas.

   - Note that student drawings can represent an example of the vocabulary word or term, the main idea of the word or term, or associations and connections to the word or term.

   - Have students work independently, in pairs, or in groups.

   - Instruct students to begin drawing only after you have described the vocabulary word or term and the students have recorded accurate descriptions of the word or term (Marzano, 2004). Otherwise, students may create false associations that do not accurately reflect the meaning of key concepts. For example, the teacher can describe a "monarch" as the ruler of a country. If the student draws a measurement ruler with a crown on it, he/she has made a false association.

ACTIVITY 23
Teach Cognates

Context:

Teacher/Students

Description:

This activity helps students identify patterns of cognates from Spanish to English by showing them examples. This helps students identify similarities and differences between Spanish and English and thus helps them reflect on what they know about language.

Directions:

1. Provide students with examples and explain how cognates may be similar in Spanish and English.

2. Put students in groups of four or five and provide them with chart paper.

3. Have each group select one or two examples in Spanish and English (*ivo/ive; oso/ous; mente/ly,* etc). Ask them to write their selection as a heading on their chart paper.

4. Have students brainstorm a list and ask them to color code the word endings to note differences as shown. Allow them to use books from the classroom library to locate more cognates.

5. Have students display their charts and add to them as more cognates are encountered in future lessons.

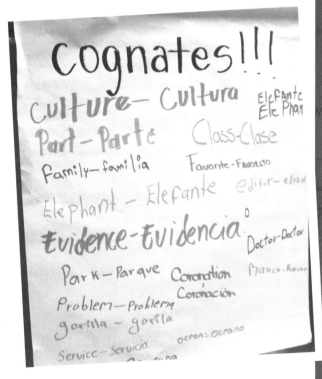

ACTIVITY 24
Teaching Morphemes

Context:

Teacher/Students, Student/Students

Description:

A morpheme is a small part of a word that has meaning and includes prefixes, suffixes, and root words. For example, the word "prereading" has three morphemes: "pre-," "read," and "-ing." These meaningful word parts are the building blocks of the academic vocabulary that students encounter in content area classrooms. Teaching morphemes gives students a tool for determining the meanings of unknown words as they encounter them in reading.

Directions: Part A

1. Become familiar with and practice using and pointing out morphemes in your classroom.

2. Introduce the concept of morphemes to students.

   - Select 2–3 common examples that students encounter regularly, like "re-" (again), "anti-" (against), and "-ology" (the study of).
   - Brainstorm words with these morphemes (e.g., reflect, antibiotic, or geology) and show students how morphemes give information about the meaning of the whole word.

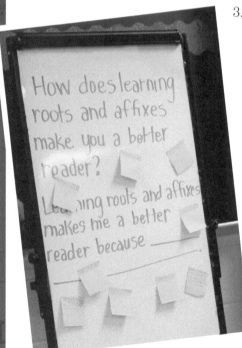

3. Teach morphemes in context by highlighting and defining morphemes found in content area and academic vocabulary. For example, "Look at the word 'chlorophyll'? Who knows what that means? That's right, it's the green material involved in photosynthesis. 'Chloro' means green, and 'phyl' means leaf."

4. Post morphemes on a word wall (see p. 110) and/or have students record them in their journals.

5. Challenge students with the "Spot the Morpheme" activity on the next page.

6. Refer to Appendix E, "List of Latin and Greek Morphemes," to guide instruction (Seidlitz & Kenfield, 2011).

Spot the Morpheme

Context:

Teacher/Students, Student/Students

Description:

Learning to detect and decipher morphemes in words is the first step toward building a better vocabulary. Students can begin to learn morphemes by recognizing Latin and Greek roots. Have your students practice using the list below.

Directions: Part B

1. Have students examine the list below.

2. Ask students to underline the morphemes in each word.

3. Provide the "List of Latin and Greek Morphemes" in Appendix E and ask students to define each morpheme. Students can work in groups to complete this activity.

biography	biology	geology	geometry
homicide	herbivorous	voracious	postscript
supervisor	intervene	submarine	homonym
photography	antibiotic	geography	
herbicide	carnivorous	scripture	
interstate	circumnavigate	pseudonym	

ACTIVITY 26

Brick and Mortar Cards

Context:

Teacher/Students, Student/Students

Description:

This activity (adapted from Zwiers, 2008) reinforces the concept that different kinds of words are needed to *build* academic understanding. There are two types of academic language: the content-specific, key vocabulary words called *brick words* and the other non-content-specific academic words called *mortar words* (Dutro & Moran, 2003). Brick words are usually boldfaced or italicized in textbooks, and teachers explicitly teach their meanings. Mortar words are general academic words that can be found in textbooks, tests, and conversations across all subject areas. They include transition words like *because, therefore*, and *additionally*, signal words like *first* or *second*, and test-specific language such as *best represents* or *based upon*. Mortar words are often abstract and without a clear definition, so the best way for students to learn these words is by using them. This activity gives students practice using the brick and mortar words they need to develop academic language.

Directions

1. List key vocabulary (brick words) from the current unit of study or select words from the word wall (see p. 110).

2. Have students (in pairs or groups) record each term on an index card or sticky note. These are the brick cards.

3. Ask students to organize the brick cards in a way that makes sense to them.

4. Ask students to link the brick words together using academic language. Students write the academic language on mortar cards (or sentence strips). These mortar cards cement the brick cards together.

5. Offer a list of mortar words and phrases to support students during this activity.

Example:

LIFE CYCLE OF THE BUTTERFLY

BRICK Cards

METAMORPHOSIS   PUPA

CATERPILLAR   CHRYSALIS   BUTTERFLY

List of **NON-CONTENT-SPECIFIC** words/phrases:

TRANSFORMS	BEGINS	EATS
NEXT	SECOND	RESTING
GROWS	LAST	STAGE
INSIDE	THEN PROCESS	IS CALLED
FIRST CHANGES INTO	FORMS	

Possible Student Responses:

A BUTTERFLY BEGINS AS A CATERPILLAR AND THEN A CHRYSALIS FORMS. IT IS NOW CALLED A PUPA AND THEN BREAKS OUT AS A BUTTERFLY. THIS PROCESS IS CALLED METAMORPHOSIS.

METAMORPHOSIS IS WHEN A CATERPILLAR TRANSFORMS INTO A BUTTERFLY. FIRST, IT IS A CATERPILLAR, THEN A PUPA INSIDE A CHRYSALIS, AND LAST A BUTTERFLY.

Teach Transition Words and Phrases

Description:

Whether you call them transition words and phrases, discourse markers, or signal words, these academic relationship indicators (*in contrast, moreover, consequently*) present a huge challenge for our newcomers. These expressions are very difficult to define and to teach out of context, and they are often ignored in our zeal to teach subject area vocabulary. But since it is unlikely that our students will learn the appropriate use of these words from inference alone, we must teach these expressions in all subject areas. They are key to both understanding academic language and to producing academic language when speaking and writing. So how can we help our students with these essential bits of academic language? Look at the chart below for a list of transitional expressions that can be organized by the cognitive task they represent. For example, the words in the second column express some kind of sequencing. Noting this classification is key to teaching these words effectively. On these two pages we offer three ways to teach signal and transition words and phrases explicitly (Seidlitz & Kenfield, 2011).

Directions:

The Language Moment

Any time you engage students in one of the cognitive tasks listed at the top of each column of the "Signal and Transition Words and Phrases" chart (description/list/generalization, sequence, comparison/contrast, cause and effect, problem/solution), continue by using the corresponding transition words. For example, after completing a step-by-step process activity such as a science lab,

SIGNAL AND TRANSITION WORDS AND PHRASES

Description/List/ Generalization	Sequence	Comparison/ Contrast	Cause and Effect Problem/Solution
for example	first, second, third	however	because
such as	in the first place	but	since
to illustrate	first of all	as well as	therefore
for instance	then before	on the other hand	consequently
in addition	after	while	as a consequence
and	last	although	in order that
again	meanwhile	different from	so that
moreover	now	less than, fewer than	as a result
also, too	finally	also, too	then
furthermore	for one thing	like	if...then
another	next	though	thus
first of all	subsequent(-ly)	much as	due to
second	later	yet	accordingly
additionally		similarly	for this reason
not only...but also		similar to	
		whereas	
		as opposed to	
		still	
		in contrast	

writers' workshop, or art project, continue by using words from the sequence column (Column 2). Say, "What did we do first? And subsequently, what did we do?" Or, if you have just compared or contrasted systems of government or characters in a story, use some compare/contrast transition words from the third column. Say, "As opposed to democracies, dictatorships discourage free expression." Or you could say, "Tim is a kind boy; on the other hand, Sally is mean." The goal is to have students independently create sentences using the signal and transition words and phrases in the context of the material you have been studying. "Language Moments" begins as an oral language activity led by the teacher, but as students use the signal and transition words at a higher level, they can create sentences with the words. Explicitly modeling the use of signal and transition words in context, in a consistent manner, is the key to success. Why does this method work? Simply put, your students have just experienced a sequential activity, or they have compared two characters, or they have learned about the causes and effects of the Civil War, and NOW their brains are primed to learn the signal and transition words and phrases that match the thinking they have done. Seize the teachable moment!

Post the Signal and Transition Words and Phrases

It is very helpful to post the "Signal and Transition Words and Phrases" chart in the classroom. Many teachers enlarge the chart on page 190 as a poster to remind students of these key words. Perhaps more importantly, it reminds the teacher to seize the teachable moment. For example, if students have just compared and contrasted states in the union, have them write sentences using compare/contrast transition words. Simply point to the transition poster and take your students on a memorable Walk 'n Talk. Use examples like, "Montana is a huge state, while Rhode Island is a tiny one" or "Similar to California, Florida has a long coastline."

Connecting Graphic Organizers with Signal and Transition Words and Phrases

Use academic language, especially signal and transition words and phrases, when working with graphic organizers. Seize the teachable moment after students complete a web, a timeline, a Venn diagram, a flow chart, or another type of graphic organizer by asking yourself, "Can this be followed by a signal or transition word language moment?" Then engage students in conversation using signal and transition words. See the examples below.

Description/List/Generalization	Sequence	Compare/Contrast	Cause and Effect Problem/Solution
Our web shows many characteristics of _____. For example...	We see that _____ occurs first. Next, _____ happens.	_____ has _____ as opposed to _____, which has _____.	_____ occurred as a result of...
Not only do we see_____, but we can also determine that...	Before _____, then _____ begins, later _____, and finally....	_____ is similar to _____ because...	_____ because... _____ is due to...

web · flow chart · timeline · cycle · Venn diagram · 3-part Venn diagram · matrix or table · cause → effect · problem · steps toward solution · solution

ACTIVITY 28
Q, Triple S, A

Context:

Teacher/Students

Description

Q, Triple S, A (or Question, Signal, Stem, Share, Assess) is an example of a structured conversation (Seidlitz & Perryman, 2011). In structured conversations, students share ideas and points of view with each other using content and language specified by the teacher.

Student–student interaction focused on lesson concepts has been shown to have a significant effect on student achievement (Marzano, Pickering, & Pollock, 2001). In this activity, every student in the class participates using academic language, and it usually takes less than a minute to implement.

Directions

- **Question:** Ask the class a question.
- **Signal:** Ask students to give you a response signal when they are ready to answer the question. Examples of response signals include showing thumbs up, giving a nod, crossing arms, etc.
- **Stem:** Provide students with a sentence stem to use when answering a question.
- **Share:** Give students the opportunity to share their responses with other students in pairs, triads, or groups.
- **Assess:** Determine the quality of student discussions and the level of student understanding.

Teachers can assess students either by randomly selecting students to share out loud or by having all students write a response.

CHAPTER 4
ENHANCE ELD INSTRUCTION

ENGLISH LANGUAGE DEVELOPMENT (ELD) INSTRUCTION involves specially designed curriculum to "advance English learners' knowledge and use of English in increasingly sophisticated ways" (Saunders, Goldenberg, & Marcelletti, 2013. p.14). Different states refer to ELD instructional courses in various ways; however, all of them focus on acquiring proficiency in English rather than focusing on mastering grade-level, content-area standards. This differs from sheltered instruction in that the entire course centers on language proficiency. Topics from content standards may be included, but they are not intended to be taught to mastery level. One consistent finding of research is that providing ELD instruction has a great impact on achievement of ELLs, and ELLs who receive high-quality ELD tend to outperform ELLs who do not (Saunders, Goldenberg, & Marcelletti, 2013). In addition, it is important for districts to make the provision of high-quality ELD instruction for newcomers a priority.

Why ESL?

What do the terms ESL, ESOL, and ELD refer to?

We certainly love our acronyms in the world of ELLs! And just to confuse things even more, the same acronym can have multiple meanings when used in different contexts. Though they may seem interchangeable on the surface, there are key intricacies that set them apart.

- ELD, English language development, is a term referring to a systematic instructional model, program, or course designed to develop the English language proficiency of ELLs.

What ELD sounds like:

-*"Our school now offers a newcomer ELD (NELD) class as an elective."*

-*"We went to a teacher conference and got some great ideas on books and materials to supplement our school's ELD resources for teachers of newcomers."*

- ESL, English as a second language, is another term that can be used to describe a program or course for ELLs—or even the students themselves. ESL classes are offered in this country (and others, such as Canada) where English is the dominant language and learners must learn the language to be able to communicate and live day-to-day in their new home country.

What ESL sounds like:

-*"Our high school ESL students are going on a field trip to the natural science museum."*

-*"The students in my church's evening adult ESL class are having a potluck dinner on Friday."*

- ESOL, English for speakers of other languages, is another term that can refer to a program or course, and it is often used interchangeably with ESL. Some learning communities in the United States prefer this term to ESL if students are bilingual in other foreign languages and are learning English as a third or fourth language instead of a second. From a K–12 context, ESOL is what will appear on a high school schedule, report card, or transcript.

What ESOL sounds like:

-*"In my school, freshmen can take ESOL I for their ELA I credit."*

-*"I am studying for my ESOL certification."*

So an **ELD** block for newcomers may consist of **ESOL I**, an **ESL** elective course, and a **NELD** elective course.

Why might newcomers need a separate English language development course (ESOL/ESL/ELD) in addition to or instead of their language arts class?

Secondary newcomers enroll at an age beyond which direct literacy instruction is typically provided to students, and most secondary teachers are not prepared to teach initial components of literacy, like phonics and fluency (Short & Boyson, 2012). **It's important to note that, in the English language arts course, the primary focus is mastery of core state standards and curricula, such as reading, analyzing, and writing about literature, and not language acquisition or development.** In some states, like Texas and Virginia, a language development course (ESOL/ESL/ELD) may be substituted for high school English language arts credit. The substituted course allows for a greater emphasis to be placed on basic language concepts (syntax, grammar, mechanics, etc.) rather than on the standard grade-level curriculum.

In conjunction with the course that fulfills the ELA requirement, newcomers can also be placed in an additional language development course to accelerate their language acquisition. Much like the courses described above, the extra language development class provides intensive foundational English language acquisition instruction in listening, speaking, reading, and writing as well as targeted instruction in vocabulary, grammar, syntax, and English mechanics. Depending on a state's course offerings, newcomers may have even further options for language development courses. In fact, it is not uncommon for high school newcomers to receive three hours of language instruction a day in order to accelerate their English language acquisition (see scheduling options on p. 157).

What is the role of the ESL Teacher?

In Chapter 3 we explored the role of the content-area teacher using language strategies to teach content to ELLs. This involved the use of high levels of comprehensible input along with linguistic accommodations in a low-stress environment. An ESL teacher, on the other hand, is primarily responsible for language development and can use the content-area concepts, among other resources, to build language. For more details, see the chart on p. 136.

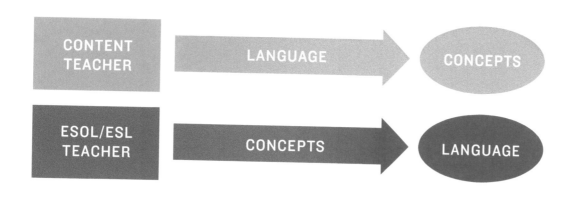

TABLE 4.1 Teacher Roles

ESL Teacher in an ESL Class	ESL Teacher in a Co-Teach Class	Content-Area Teacher in a Sheltered Class
Primary focus: English language structures and vocabulary	Primary focus: Linguistic accommodations of the subject matter for ELLs	Primary focus: Making content comprehensible for ELLs
Facilitate student interaction to develop oral language proficiency with specific English structures	Facilitate student interaction to develop oral language proficiency in the content area	Facilitate student interaction to develop oral language proficiency in the content area
Directly teaches high frequency social and academic English vocabulary	Teach academic and social English vocabulary related to lesson content	Teach academic English vocabulary related to lesson content
Provide daily opportunities for reading: teacher-selected and self-selected texts	Provide frequent opportunities for reading adapted texts related to content-area topics	Provide opportunities for reading adapted texts related to content-area topics
Provide daily instruction on specific language structures and opportunities to write using those structures	Provide linguistically accommodated opportunities to write about content-related topics	Provide linguistically accommodated opportunities to write about content-related topics

How can the ESL teacher and the content-area teacher collaborate effectively?

When I first started out teaching newcomers (and had no idea what I was doing), the ESL teachers on the team, Alfonso Vazquez and Jeanna McCulla, were truly instrumental in helping me find my way. I took advantage of every opportunity I had to pick their brains, peek into their classes, observe them teaching, take note of the layout and physical environment of their classrooms, and most importantly, observe the students. I vividly remember being completely amazed at how the students performed in these ESL classes for these two teachers and how vastly different the students' participation, understanding, and genuine engagement looked compared to those same students in my class. It was a paradigm shift for me. I was a sponge; I listened and took in everything the teachers said and did. I tried, to the best of my ability, to adapt those techniques and methods and incorporate them into my biology class. Although I was trained in sheltered instruction by this point, figuring out how to actually implement those strategies into all I was taught was at times overwhelming. However, seeing what high-quality instruction for ELLs looked liked was a game changer for me. In fact, I credit much of the success I had with my ELLs and newcomer ELLs to the strong relationship I had with the ESL teachers on my team.

*TAKE NOTE

The ESL teacher can be a remarkable resource for the content-area teacher.

Read below for more ideas and reflections on the roles of ESL and content-area teachers:

- ESL and content-area teachers are encouraged to team together and dedicate planning or conference time to talk about students, language levels, common celebrations, etc.

- ESL teachers can provide ideas and feedback on instructional, linguistic, and assessment accommodations.

- ESL teachers are often most knowledgeable regarding planning and implementing scaffolded instruction for ELLs. Content-area teachers can watch, observe, and talk to ESL teachers for recommended best practices.

- ESL teachers can provide advice on materials and texts that can supplement what the content-area teacher is already using.

- ESL teachers can provide clarification on language proficiency levels.

- ESL teachers can provide advice on simplifying language and differentiating activities.

- ESL teachers can review content and vocabulary during the ESL elective class. (In my case, students had their interactive notebooks and all the material I front-loaded for them, and they would review it as a class with Mr. Vazquez, the ESL teacher. He would then use the same vocabulary and reinforce concepts with the students.)

- ESL teachers work with students in smaller settings and often know more about students' strengths and weaknesses, family and personal histories, and other insights into the students that can be useful for content-area teachers.

- ESL teachers can provide support and feedback for content-area teachers as they implement sheltered instruction practices and begin embedding them into their daily instruction.

What are some things to avoid when coordinating between ESL and content-area teachers?

Although ESL teachers are primarily responsible for a newcomer's language acquisition, they play a supportive role in a student's content-knowledge attainment. It is the content-area teacher's responsibility to ensure that lessons are comprehensible and effectively accommodated for the newcomer's language proficiency level. The ESL teacher can certainly offer assistance and guidance in this realm; however, ESL and newcomer classes should not be viewed as study hall or homework help, as they are places where language and vocabulary building take precedence. It is recommended that content-area teachers do not merely send ESL students "down the hall to the ESL teacher" because of perceived gaps in understanding. These students will benefit instead from being immersed in a language-rich environment where content is comprehensible and language learning strategies are embedded within content-area instruction.

LUCY DESCRIBED FEELING ISOLATED IN AT LEAST ONE OF HER CLASSES: HER ELECTIVE COURSE,

ROTC. She told me how the instructor would leave the ESL students alone in a different classroom while he worked with the non-ESL students. Lucy explained, "They put you apart in a different classroom. They didn't talk to you." Changing the tone of her voice to mimic her ROTC instructor, Lucy continued, "They're learning English so, poor babies, leave them on the other side [of the room]." She further explained that the instructor would occasionally send a Spanish-speaking student over to the ESL group to check on them but, as Lucy explained with a laugh and a big smile, "They would just play with us and speak Spanish with us...I think that doesn't help a lot."

ESL Curriculum and Instruction

What curriculum options and resources are available for teaching ESOL/ESL/ELD to newcomers?

There are three basic curriculum options available for teaching ESOL/ESL/ELD to newcomers:

- Using state-adopted textbooks
- Adapting grade level ELAR (English Language Arts and Reading) curriculum.
- Creating curriculum based on state language and/or content standards

TABLE 4.2 Curriculum Options

Curriculum Option	Benefits	Challenges	Resources
State-Adopted Textbooks	Integrate state ESL/ESOL/ELD standards Align to all language proficiency levels Include a variety of ancillary materials (newcomer resource packets, visuals, etc.) May be designed as a supplementary course in addition to grade-level ELAR course	Pose difficulties in directly aligning with ELAR curriculum Require more work in preparing newcomers for transition to mainstream ELAR classes Limit opportunities for aligning learning to student culture and interests	Student textbook Teacher's edition of textbook Student workbook(s) Other ancillary materials Corresponding online materials Newcomer resource packets
Adapted Language Arts Curriculum	Allows for easy transition of newcomers into mainstream ELAR classes Ensures grade-level curriculum for newcomers Boosts newcomers self-confidence by showing them they can study the same content as mainstream students	Requires extensive time and effort to adapt texts Needs significant alterations of pace of instructional delivery Includes few, if any, specially designed materials tailored to newcomers' needs	English language arts textbook, anthologies, short stories, novels, and poetry Teacher guides to literary works Outlines, notes, and study guides related to content Spanish-language resources provided through ELAR textbook Versions of literary works in newcomers' home language Summaries in newcomers' home language
Teacher Created Curriculum	Facilitates design of material according to students' background, culture, and needs Enables opportunities for shared writing Provides space for high-interest, experience-based approaches to instruction Allows teacher to tailor curriculum to student and teacher preferences/interests May be designed as a supplementary course in addition to grade-level ELAR course	Requires time and effort to find materials and create experiences Demands greater time and effort to ensure that learning experiences are aligned to language and/or content standards Calls for in-depth knowledge of ESL/ESOL/ELD standards, as well as familiarity with standards of other content areas	High interest, low reading level books Professional resources related to understanding Language Experience Approach (Nessel & Dixon, 2008) Professional resources related to Reader's and Writer's Workshop (Buly, 2010) Professional resources related to integrating technology with English language development

What does an effective ESL lesson that promotes ELD include?

The most important thing for an ESL teacher to remember is to focus the instruction on providing sufficient amounts of comprehensible input and opportunities with an environment that promotes a low affective filter (see p.79). An effective ESL lesson will include the following components:

- Posted content and language objectives
- Evidence of explicit vocabulary instruction
- Evidence of teacher using a variety of techniques to make content comprehensible
- Evidence of reading and writing in academic English
- Evidence of student–student interaction focusing on lesson concepts
- Specific instructional interventions for ELLs appropriate to students' language levels (e.g., sentence stems, native language resources, word banks, low-risk environment for language production).

The ESL classroom should include content and language objectives that are clearly stated near the beginning of a lesson. Content objectives in an ESL lesson could either be aligned with language arts standards or the topic of the texts being used during the lesson. Language objectives should be clearly defined and aligned to the state language standards. The language objectives selected should provide a significant language practice opportunity for the students and should be the focus of the teacher's energy. While students will listen, speak, read, and write in every lesson, the language objective will be introduced and assessed.

Teachers may need to unpack specific vocabulary found in the objectives to ensure students understand the language. Language objectives will often include sentence stems that are sometimes differentiated by proficiency levels. After introducing the objective, teachers should introduce concepts, words, and phrases that students will be using and will find in the text they are going to read. This can be done using visuals, gestures, native language resources and vocabulary activities as needed.

A variety of techniques throughout the lesson must be used to ensure the language is comprehensible to the students. Teachers will make sure to give clear, simple directions (see Point and Talk, p.118) and use strategies such as choral response, rephrasing, and response signals while explaining instructional tasks to the students. It is important to prompt students to participate in student–student conversations in English by providing sentence stems, modeling, and using specific activities (see TPR Storytelling, p. 153).

Teachers need to select texts for students to read that will be comprehensible to the students, yet provide an opportunity to expand their language development. The texts should be readable, yet some words and language structures should be new to the students. Student conversations and writings should be either directly or indirectly related to the texts. The text the ESL teacher selects for reading can be an ESL textbook, a content-area textbook, or another source. Sometimes the teacher may need to provide a simplified text, a native-language glossary, or a native-language summary for students at lower levels of proficiency, especially in a heterogeneous class. Teachers may model the pronunciation and explain the meaning of challenging vocabulary before students read a text.

The following activities can be used to help students before and during reading in an ESL class:

- After reading, students should be provided with stems to help them discuss and write about what they have read.
- For students at lower levels of proficiency, teachers will provide more structure for students' writing, such as cloze sentences, charts, and organizers.
- For students at higher levels of proficiency, writing tasks are more open-ended and can involve more complex grammatical structures.
- At the end of the lesson, content and language objectives should be reviewed and informally or formally assessed.
- In addition to teacher-selected texts, time for student-selected reading should be a significant portion of an ESL class. This time should be structured so that students have an opportunity to reflect on what they are reading and discuss it with other students.

In Appendix B (p. 171) and Appendix C (p. 173) of this book, you will find a myriad of resources to enhance and supplement ESL/ELD instruction.

How can I support a newcomer developing L1 literacy?

If the students have higher levels of literacy in their L1/home language, teachers may subscribe to World Book Online to search for an academic topic that can automatically be translated by selecting from a list of 30-plus available world languages. Additionally, encourage students to read in their L1 (during Free Voluntary Reading, SSR, or DEAR time), as newcomers who are highly efficient in their L1 tend to be more successful at acquiring English at a faster rate (Goldenberg & Coleman, 2010). To encourage free voluntary reading in the L1, libraries or bookstores such as Half Price Books may have books in less-commonly known world languages that you can obtain for the students as they grow a biliteracy practice.

Developing students' writing is equally important. Allowing newcomers to journal, pre-write, and brainstorm in the L1 results in higher-quality writing in L2 (the second/target language) in later stages of the writing process (Yigsaw, 2012). For newcomers, allowing students to write in their L1 is a research-based accommodation that can lead to academic gains.

When talking about L1 literacy, it is also important to keep in mind that newcomers can be literate in their L1 at various levels. The purpose of the following chart is to familiarize you with those levels and to offer instructional suggestions and considerations for each newcomer's unique needs.

TABLE 4.3 Type of L1 Literacy and Effects on L2 Literacy Learning

L1 literacy	Explanation	Special considerations
Preliterate	L1 has no written form (Indigenous American, African, Australian, and Pacific languages).	Learners need exposure to the purposes and use of literacy.
Nonliterate	Learners had no access to literacy instruction.	Learners may feel stigmatized.
Semiliterate	Learners had limited access to literacy instruction.	Learners may have had past negative experiences with literacy learning.
Nonalphabet literate	Learners are fully literate in a language written in a nonalphabetic script such as Chinese.	Learners need instruction in reading and alphabetic script and in sound–syllable correspondents in English.
Non-Roman alphabet literate	Learners are literate in a language written in a non-Roman alphabet (Arabic, Greek, Korean, Russian, or Thai).	Learners need instruction in the Roman alphabet to transfer their L1 literacy skills to English. Some readers (e.g., Arabic) will need to learn to read from left to right.
Roman-alphabet literate	Learners are fully literate in a language written in a Roman-alphabet script (French, German, or Spanish).	Learners need instruction in the specific letter-to-sound and sound–syllable correspondents of English.

Note. Reprinted from *Reading and the adult English learner: A review of the research.* (p.13), Burt, M., Peyton, J.K. & Adams, R., 2003, Washington, D.C.: Copyright 2003 by Center for Applied Linguistics.

What are some terms and concepts often found in ESL curricula that ESL teachers need to be aware of ?

TABLE 4.4 ESL/Linguistics Terminology

Term	Description	Example
Phoneme/Phonology	Distinct units of sound in a specified language that distinguish one word from another	*m, b, t,* and *p* in the English words "mop," "bop," "top," and "pop"
Morpheme/Morphology	A meaningful unit of a language that cannot be further divided	"Forth," "come," and "ing" in "forthcoming"
Syntax	Arrangement of words and phrases to create well-formed sentences in a language	Incorrect syntax: "The customer's car we repaired was very pleased and called me later to thank me."
Semantics	Meaning of a word, phrase, sentence, or text	Dog: a domesticated, carnivorous mammal that typically has a long snout, an acute sense of smell, and a barking, howling, or whining voice
Denotation	The literal or primary meaning of a word	Cheap: low in price Inexpensive: low in price Economical: low in price
Connotation	An idea or feeling that a word invokes	"Servant" versus "housekeeper," or "sanitation worker" versus "trash man"
Homophone	A word that is pronounced the same as another word but differs in meaning and may differ in spelling	to, too, two jean, gene karat, carat, caret, carrot
Polysemy	The coexistence of many possible meanings for a word or phrase	bright deposit
Graphophonics	The system of the relationship between sounds and letters; patterns in a language	tion - /shun/ ould - /ood/
Pragmatics	The use of language in social contexts and the ways in which people produce and comprehend meanings	Teaching students to take turns talking in a conversation
Lexicon	Collection of words—the internalized dictionary that every speaker of a language has	Teachers have their own lexicon: C&I, ARDS, differentiation and scaffolding, ELD, LEP, ESL, ELL
Discourse	Written or spoken communication	Students discussing or writing about a short story they just read

ACTIVITY 28
Morpheme Games

Context:

Teacher/Students, Student/Students

Description:

Working with morphemes helps students realize that words can be "figured out" by carefully examining word parts. When students discover that the meaning of a morpheme can help them uncover the definition of a long and challenging word, listening, speaking, reading, and writing immediately become easier tasks to handle. Part A, "Morpheme Matching," lets students flex their morpheme muscles by using morphemes in a creative way. Part B, "Which one means...?" gives students advanced practice with morpheme recognition. The two activities can also be used to assess how well students understand various word parts (Seidlitz & Kenfield, 2011).

Directions:

PART A: Morpheme Matching

1. Provide a list of morphemes for students.
   - Begin with a list of a few morphemes, and increase the quantity of the list as students become more skilled at using them.
   - Always include morphemes related to current classroom vocabulary.
   - Include the definitions for the morphemes if they are new to students. If students have had multiple exposures to the morphemes, they may not need the definitions.
   - It may be helpful to divide the morpheme list into prefixes, roots, and suffixes.

2. Ask students to create words using the morphemes from the list, either individually or in pairs. The words can be actual words or made-up words (since the purpose of this activity is practice and manipulation of morphemes, creating actual words is not crucial).

3. Use the created words by:
   - writing a definition for each word based upon the meanings of the morphemes;
   - sharing the words with other students; and/or
   - asking other students to guess the meaning of the created words.

Morpheme List (without definitions)

pre-	read	-scope
auto-	hydro	-graph
photo-	geo	-ology
sub-	duo	-ist

Possible Student Responses:

1. Readology: the study of reading

2. Hydroscope: tool that observes water

3. Subgeology: the study of things under the Earth

4. Photoist: someone who believes in light

5. Autograph: writing about myself

6. Duoist: someone who does everything twice

PART B: Which one means..?

1. Compile a list of words that share a common morpheme. Display the list for students to see. Examples include:

_____scope	pre_____	___bio___
microscope	preapprove	antibiotic
telescope	precaution	biographer
gyroscope	predetermine	symbiotic
kaleidoscope	preface	microbiology
periscope	prepare	biodegradable

2. Read the definition for one of the words on the list.

3. Instruct students to apply their knowledge of morphemes to connect the definition with the correct word. Provide the following sentence stem to improve the quality of responses:

"I think the word is _____ because I know the morpheme _____ means …."

ACTIVITY 29
Reader's Theatre

Context:

Teacher/Students, Students/Students

Description:

This is a technique widely used by language teachers to help students grow in elements of oral language fluency, including phrasing, smoothness, pace, juncture, intonation, and stress. The technique does not require the use of props and can be very engaging for ELLs (Seidlitz, Base, Lara, & Smith, 2016).

Directions:

1. Select a script. The script should have a story and characters that will be interesting to the students. Popular fairy tales can be a source of humor and cultural knowledge for students. You may also want to look for scripts that reflect the students' culture and experiences. You may wish to have advanced students collaborate on writing a script. Either record yourself reading the script or read the script aloud with the students. Then choose who will read which part or have students self-select their parts in small groups.

2. Review vocabulary with the students. Preview the script and pre-teach vocabulary that may be challenging.

3. Students rehearse the parts. They need to practice their parts several times, either inside or outside of class. The focus is not on "reading" but on creating a quality performance. Students may add sound effects to their performance if appropriate.

4. The students perform the play. Performance should be simple and without props or costumes. Sometimes bringing in an outside audience or recording the performance can enhance student engagement and involvement. They can be evaluated on the basis of volume, pronunciation, posture, eye contact, smoothness, and intonation.

Some suggested scripts can be found in the following: *12 Fabulously Funny Folktale Plays or 12 Fabulously Funny Fairy Tale Plays* by Justin McCory Martin, *Reader's Theater Scripts (Secondary)* by Gail S. Hennessey, *Teatro: Hispanic Plays for Young People* by Angel Vigil, and *Aplauso: Hispanic Children's Theater* by Joe Rosenburg.

ACTIVITY 30

Strategic TV

Context:

Student/Self, Student/Student

Description:

Through guided discussion and demonstration, the teacher explains how students can use television and video to help them learn the target language more rapidly (Seidlitz, Base, Lara, & Smith, 2016).

Directions:

1. Explain the concept of comprehensible input to your students, highlighting the fact that the more comprehensible input they receive in the target language, the faster they will develop proficiency in that language. Also explain the concept of compelling input, highlighting the fact that the more compelling people find the content, the more likely they are to watch it attentively.

2. Demonstrate to students how to watch TV and video strategically in order to increase comprehensible and compelling input, outlining the following key ideas:

   • Input will increase the more you understand the program you're watching.

   • Programs in which you have a high degree of interest are more likely to capture your attention and keep you watching for longer periods of time.

   • Watching recordings that you can pause and/or replay can increase comprehensible input. However, pausing too frequently can interrupt the flow necessary to receive large amounts of comprehensible input.

   • Utilizing closed captioning with the target language printed on the bottom of the screen can increase the amount of comprehensible input a viewer is receiving.

   • Some programs available online specialize in providing video-based comprehensible input for language learners (for example, YABLA).

3. Provide a log for students to record the number of minutes watched and the programs viewed. You may wish to assign a particular genre of programming or a specific number of minutes for students to watch per day.

4. Provide opportunities in class for students to discuss the programs they are watching with one another, with the teacher, or with the entire class. Using sentence stems, students can speak or write about their experiences using Strategic TV.

ACTIVITY 31

Embedded Reading

Context:

Teacher/Self, Teacher/Students

Description:

In their respective work, Blaine Ray and Stephen Krashen encourage teachers to ensure that ELLs have access to engaging reading texts. In order for beginner/intermediate ELLs to read complex material, certain adjustments to texts are necessary. Embedded Reading is a way of adapting text that enables students, especially those at lower levels of language proficiency, to receive comprehensible input while gaining access to and comprehending grade-level text(Seidlitz, Base, Lara, & Smith, 2016).

Directions:

1. Choose a grade-level text you want beginning or intermediate students to be able to read and comprehend. The text should be approximately 250 to 750 words.

2. Write a simpler version of the text line-by-line, simplifying clauses, removing adjectives and adverbs, and replacing lower-frequency vocabulary with higher-frequency vocabulary. This will become the intermediate level text. For example, the sentence from Romeo and Juliet, "Two households both alike in dignity in fair Verona where we lay our scene," would be rewritten as, "There were two households in Verona. Both households had dignity. This is where our scene takes place."

3. Rewrite the simplified version again, further simplifying the text. This is the beginner level text. Make sure to eliminate complex clauses, and to use repetitive grammatical structures as frequently as possible. For example, "There were two households in Verona. The two households were important. The two households are in this scene."

4. Give the students the simplest (beginner) text to read. They should scan the text for unfamiliar vocabulary, and you can provide the meanings of those words.

5. Have the students read the intermediate text. Provide meanings for unfamiliar words they find through their scanning of the text.

6. Repeat this process using the original text, making sure to provide meanings for unfamiliar words.

7. Expect the students to struggle with grammatical structures and meanings of words in the grade-level text. The goal is not to achieve complete comprehension of every aspect of the text, but to gain a general understanding of the text and to receive grade-level comprehensible input.

ACTIVITY 32

Movin' On Up Reading

Context:

Teacher/Students

Description:

As teachers of ELLs, we are aware that one of the most significant things we can do to improve our students' performance is to increase their reading proficiency. We are also aware of the impact moving ahead in their reading has on their English-language proficiency rating and their overall performance on state assessments. But how do we do this? In order to increase students' reading proficiency in English, we must remember one of the key principles related to comprehensible input: the amount counts. We must find ways to increase their reading in content-area classes and outside of class. Through this activity for students in third grade or higher, we can discover a structured process for increasing our ELLs' reading stamina and proficiency (Seidlitz, Base, Lara, & Smith, 2016).

Directions:

1. Have students read a short, comprehensible, content-related text, one paragraph in length, followed by accountable conversation in any content-area class. If students are not successful, make sure that they have sufficient background knowledge and English language fluency to read the paragraph you selected.

2. Within two or three days, have students read a slightly longer text followed by accountable conversation. Make sure all students have read the text with comprehension. The key here is for all students to be successful in reading, comprehending, and discussing a content-related text.

3. In two or three days, have students read a longer text, again followed by accountable conversation. Continue to monitor to be sure struggling readers are successful at comprehending and discussing the text with their peers.

4. Gradually increase the time students read until they are able to read content-area text for 30 to 60 minutes silently with comprehension. This may sound like a lot; however, the reading they do on the state assessments takes longer than 30 to 60 minutes. If they are unaccustomed to reading silently about academic content for extended periods, they will be like someone running a marathon without ever running even 13 miles. This is not an activity in which students will engage on a daily basis, but it is important that ELLs practice silently reading content-related text for extended periods somewhat frequently prior to a benchmark or a state assessment.

ACTIVITY 33

Movin' On Up Writing

Context:

Teacher/Students, Student/Student

Description:

In order to advance in writing proficiency, students need opportunities to write, not only in their language arts and ESL classes, but also in content-area classes. Students need frequent opportunities to write about what they have read and discussed in class. This activity is designed to provide a framework that can help students advance in their writing proficiency on both the English language proficiency rating and state assessments. It involves using particular stems and structures in content-area classes so that students frequently write with greater levels of English language proficiency (Seidlitz, Base, Lara, & Smith, 2016).

Directions:

1. Have students read and annotate a content-related text on a particular topic.

2. Have students discuss the topic with a partner as a structured conversation (Q, Triple S, A).

3. Write a question for the students to respond to in paragraph form. The question should be related to the text, and the response should begin with a sentence stem.

4. Provide students with a specific set of transition words they can use when writing their paragraph from the Signal and Transition Word guide at right.

5. Tell students they will be writing a one-paragraph response to the question. The paragraph should include the following:

   • A sentence stem

   • Three or more additional sentences

   • At least two transition words from the Signal and Transition Word guide.

6. Show students two sample paragraphs you have written: an example and a non-example. Your sample text should not be about the exact topic on which the students are going to write, but should be a related topic that could use similar stems in transition words. In the non-example, include common student errors such as capitalization errors, incorrect spelling, incomplete sentences, incomplete thoughts, subject–verb agreement errors, and lack of coherence. In the example, show students the kind of writing you would expect from a highly proficient student who understands the topic well.

7. Have students write their paragraphs.

8. When assessing the paragraphs, look for clear understanding of the content and proficient use of English using the English language proficiency rating descriptors.

9. Note common content-area and language mistakes made by the students. The next time a writing assignment is given, you can use some of the typical student mistakes in a new non-example that you create, and you can model correct language usage for the students.

SIGNAL AND TRANSITION WORDS AND PHRASES

Description/List/ Generalization	Sequence	Comparison/ Contrast	Cause and Effect Problem/Solution
for example	first, second,	however	because
such as	third	but	since
to illustrate	in the first place	as well as	therefore
for instance	first of all	on the other hand	consequently
in addition	then before	while	as a consequence
and	after	although	in order that
again	last	different from	so that
moreover	meanwhile	less than, fewer than	as a result
also, too	now	also, too	then
furthermore	finally	like	if…then
another	for one thing	though	thus
first of all	next	much as	due to
second	subsequent(-ly)	yet	accordingly
additionally	later	similarly	for this reason
not only…but also		similar to	
		whereas	
		as opposed to	
		still	
		in contrast	

ACTIVITY 34

Language Experience Approach

Context:

Teacher/Students

Description:

LEA is an approach to literacy that involves a teacher eliciting stories and experiences from a student or group of students. Examples of shared experiences could be class field trips, cultural/holiday programs in schools, lessons from a guest speaker, etc. As the stories and experiences are shared, the teacher or tutor transcribes the students' experiences. These transcriptions then become texts that the students and other students in the learning community use as literacy-building texts. It is important that the communication between the students and teacher is as natural as possible and that the topic chosen for the activity is relevant and encouraging to all students as a shared classroom experience. The key for a successful LEA is to use students' own vocabulary, language patterns, and shared experiences to create texts that make the reading process meaningful and enjoyable (Nessel & Dixon, 2008).

Directions:

The five steps for conducting an LEA:

Language Skill	LEA Step
Speaking and Listening	**Step 1:** Discuss a shared experience, such as a field trip or classroom project.
Composing (Oral)	**Step 2:** As students discuss the experience in their own words, the teacher reframes their statements, recording their thoughts on chart paper for all students to see. At this point, students are connecting oral to written language by seeing their own thoughts and words recorded on paper.
Listening and Reading	**Step 3:** Once constructed, the teacher reads the text out loud to the students, modeling the sounds of the language with expression. Then with the teacher's help, students practice reading the text several times.
Developing Reading/Word Recognition	**Step 4:** The teacher guides the students in recognizing specific words and aids in their development of reading skills, such as determining meaning from context, phonics, and structures of the language.
Writing	**Step 5:** Students then use the shared text as a springboard for writing original compositions.

ACTIVITY 35

TPR Storytelling

Context:

Teacher/Students

Description:

Using TPR Storytelling, the teacher guides and facilitates the collaborative creation of a story with the students. Language teachers such as Blaine Ray and Ben Slavic developed this technique as a way of focusing on maximizing comprehensible input. Students learn new structures and vocabulary as the teacher embeds specific structures and vocabulary into the story.

Directions:

1. The first step is to establish meaning. Select two to three new phrases that will comprise the core of the story and post these phrases or stems so they are clearly visible to the students. For example: "___ has/does not have _____." "___ wants/does not want ____." "___ goes to____." Pronounce and clearly explain the meaning of the stems to the students. Then ask the students personal questions using the stems. For example, "Does Brian have…?" "Does Carlos want…?" "Does Lee go…?"

2. The second step is to create a spoken class story. Do not tell the story yourself, but rather ask the students for the story. The stems will be repeated over and over as you ask the students about what happens to the character or characters next. Stems are often repeated between 50 and 100 times during this process. Students tend to remain engaged because of the humor in anticipation generated by the process of deciding what happens next and contributing to the co-creation process from their own funds of knowledge and cultural framework.

   For example:
   Teacher: Linda does not have a dog. Linda does not have a cat. Linda does not have a hamster. What does Linda have, Leo?

   Leo: Linda has an alpaca.

   Teacher: Linda has an alpaca. Does Linda want an alpaca? No, Linda does not want an alpaca. Linda wants… What does Linda want, Hernando?

   Hernando: Linda wants a gerbil.

3. The third step is for students to read a text containing the structures that they practiced. You may wish to read the story aloud and then have students work with a partner to translate the story or discuss its meaning in their native language. The goal is for students to have total comprehensibility of the passage.

Literature Circles

Context:
Student/Students

Description:
Literature circles in groups of four or six are also a great way to get students working in teams.

Directions:
1. Have sets of four books available.
2. Let students choose their own book.
3. Form teams based on students' choices of books.
4. Encourage readers to use notes, post-its, and discussion questions to analyze their books.
5. Have teams conduct discussions about their books.
6. Have teams share what they read with the whole class.
7. Facilitate further discussion with the whole class on each of the books.
8. For the next literature circle, students select new books.

CHAPTER 5
SCHEDULE *for* SUCCESS

AS A CLASSROOM TEACHER, you may have glanced at the title of this chapter and assumed that it is not for you, but for the counselors, registrars, administrators, and other newcomer stakeholders. Not so! If you are a teacher with any number of newcomers, those learners are spending the most critical hours of their days with you in your classroom. You have the opportunity to establish rapport with your students and learn from their unique backgrounds and educational histories. Oftentimes, newcomers will be able to share much more with you, their teacher, than they will someone in a more administrative role. You are in a position to glean valuable insights into the lives of these students, and you can advocate on their behalf when it comes to scheduling for success, given your knowledge of their past academic experiences and abilities. The sections in this chapter serve to provide you with further insights into these experiences and how they can be useful for determining grade placement and scheduling and awarding credit based on (or despite a lack of) transcripts. You can also learn more about the structure of newcomer centers and how resources can be more effectively allocated for teacher-preparedness.

Grade Placement, Scheduling, and Credits

PRIOR TO IMMIGRATING TO THE UNITED STATES, LUCY HAD GRADUATED FROM HIGH SCHOOL in Colombia at 15 years old and had begun studying psychology at the local university. She completed two semesters at the university before she and her family moved to the United States. Upon arrival in the country, Lucy wanted to continue studying at the college level, but her exceedingly limited English proficiency made that unfeasible. Lucy knew some basic vocabulary and could understand some simple sentences. Lucy's aunt, who was a teacher's assistant in another district, suggested that Lucy enroll in high school so that she could learn more English and prepare better for college. Lucy's aunt also pointed out that getting a high school diploma from the United States would make getting into college easier since her high school and college paperwork and transcripts from Colombia would not have to be translated.

Lucy explained that when she went to enroll at the local high school, school personnel informed her that she would be classified as a freshman. This was quite upsetting to Lucy. "When I went to Henderson [the local high school] I got frustrated when they told me that I have to go back to be a freshman. I was like, 'Oh my gosh, four more years!' I was in the university [in Colombia], and to go back to the ninth grade… It was really frustrating. I start crying like, 'Oh my God, I don't want to go back to the ninth grade! Four more years, and then what about my career?'"

This was a challenge for Lucy because, even with her limited English proficiency, she found the material being taught in her freshmen courses and ESL class to be basic and undemanding.

The assistant principal at Henderson, who oversaw the ESL program, advocated for Lucy and began to look for ways to accelerate her completion of high school. A solution was created in which Henderson would grant credits to Lucy based on her Colombian high school transcript if she could demonstrate enough English proficiency and content knowledge to pass the state's exit-level achievement test. Lucy began working closely with a team of teachers after school to receive additional help with both her English skills and content mastery. Eventually, Lucy passed a practice exit-level exam and was granted a sufficient number of credits to be classified as a senior following the end of her sophomore year. Lucy happily explained, "I felt so much better because everything was moving on."

What are some options when scheduling newcomers?

Scheduling options for newcomers vary widely and are limited only by a school's or district's resources, creativity, and flexibility. In order to meet the needs of newcomer students, especially those in middle and high school who need to learn enough English to earn academic credits and graduate in a short period of time, flexible and creative scheduling is crucial. This often means adjustments and alternatives to the mainstream school schedules and academic programs. Some examples of this may include the following:

Block scheduling

- Multiple courses taken sequentially in the day so that newcomers have a block of time dedicated to language acquisition

Smaller class sizes

- Smaller classes benefit newcomers in a number of ways since they allow for more personal contact and closer communication between teacher and student, thus limiting opportunities for students to be overlooked (Zvoch, 2006).

Granting extra learning time

- Extended school days, summer school, Saturday school, and/or vacation institutes or camps

Self-contained classes

- Similar to an elementary school model, a teacher covers all (or the most critical) subject areas. I once observed a high school newcomer program where the same teacher taught ESOL, ESL, a math, and a science block to the same group of newcomers. More than 20 years ago, Legters, McDill, and McPartland (1994) maintained that self-contained classrooms allow the teacher and student to become well-acquainted, provide opportunities for more individual attention, and afford the teacher a better opportunity to identify students' strengths and weaknesses.

Looping

- Looping is an innovative practice that can contribute to the success of newcomers, providing the students with consistency by having the same teacher or teachers instruct the same group of students for two or more years in a row. For example, students may have the same ELA teacher for ESOL I and then ESOL II the following year, and another teacher for IPC one year and biology the next. The math teacher may teach algebra I, then geometry the following year, and so on. Of course, a third year could be added, but finding teachers certified in multiple grade levels and/or multiple content areas could be challenging.

Co-teaching models

- In this scheduling model, two teachers are assigned to the same group of students in the same class period and support each other to address both content and language development. For example, a reading teacher and science teacher could be paired to teach a block of ELD and science. The reading teacher utilizes best practices for reading and vocabulary development while the content teacher addresses the content standards. Students would receive credit for both the reading course and the science course while receiving instruction from both experts.

Things to consider:

- Determine students' needs and design schedules and structures to meet those needs. This may mean that different newcomers have different schedules, especially those who come with credits from their home country.

- Scheduling can be based on proficiency levels or grade levels (example: different sections of ESL/ELD based on proficiency levels).

- Newcomers may need more sections of ESL/ELD than students at other proficiency levels.

- Newcomer language courses, such as ESL/ELD, need a stronger focus on literacy development and should provide more explicit instruction in English grammar, syntax, vocabulary, and mechanics.

- Small-group instruction (stations) and individualized, computer-based learning can accommodate multiple grade levels and students with various levels of academic background knowledge and language levels in the same classroom.

- An additional study skills or tutoring class (often taught by an ESL teacher or master SI teacher) is an excellent elective option.

The following examples illustrate the various and flexible scheduling options for newcomers.

Middle School Examples

MIDDLE SCHOOL A

Newcomer Reading/ELA/Newcomer ELD block (6th, 7th, 8th grade cohort)

Newcomer Math per grade level (stations/small-group instruction to meet the needs of students with various levels of academic background)

Newcomer Science per grade level (stations/small-group instruction to meet the needs of students with various levels of academic background)

All other classes grade-level SI mainstream*

*specialized, highly trained ELL team for each grade level; classes are heterogeneously mixed with LEP students (including newcomers) and non-LEP students, and all teams utilize SI strategies effectively and consistently

---

MIDDLE SCHOOL B

Students placed in age-appropriate grade cohort (6th, 7th, 8th grade cohort)

A/B block on alternative days

A block: ESL literacy/ELD block with an ESL/social studies content focus

B block: ESL literacy/ELD block with an ESL/math/science content focus

Computer class (grade-level SI mainstream)

Elective (grade-level SI mainstream)

PE (grade-level SI mainstream)

Middle School C

Newcomer Reading/ELA/Newcomer ELD block (all grades mixed in the same class, with sub-groups by proficiency level)

Newcomer Math (school-created curriculum covering all grade levels)

Newcomer Science (school-created curriculum covering all grade levels)

Social Studies (grade-level SI mainstream)

PE (grade-level SI mainstream)

Elective (grade-level SI mainstream)

MIDDLE SCHOOL D

Newcomer Reading/ELA block per grade level

All other classes grade-level SI mainstream

High School Examples

High school schedules have less flexibility and may be a bit more complex, as one must balance credits earned from the home country, any credits still needed for graduation requirements, and the individual language needs of the students.

HIGH SCHOOL A

Full-day newcomer schedule

ELD/ESOL/Reading block: two sections based on proficiency levels

Newcomer Science (IPC or Biology)

Newcomer Math (Algebra I or Geometry)

Newcomer Computer Literacy

Newcomer Speech (follows high school speech curriculum with an emphasis on oral language development)

HIGH SCHOOL B

ELA/Newcomer Reading/ELD block

Utilizes state-approved ESL textbook and newcomer curriculum

Newcomer Algebra I for those without credits (students with credits from home country go to next-level math)

Newcomer IPC for those without credits (students with credits from home country go to next-level science)

All other classes grade-level SI mainstream*

*specialized, highly trained ELL team for each grade level; classes are heterogeneously mixed with LEP students (including newcomers) and non-LEP students, and all teams utilize SI strategies effectively and consistently

High School C

All LEP students scheduled the same—no specialized course for newcomers except for ELA

ESOL I/Reading block: ninth grade (for students in first two years in U.S. schools), follows a modified English I curriculum

ESOL II/Reading block: 10th grade (for students in first two years in U.S. schools), follows a modified English II curriculum

All others grade-level ELA courses

All other classes grade-level SI mainstream

High School D

Triple block (three classes) of ESOL/Reading/ELD

Newcomer Algebra I

Newcomer Geometry

Newcomer Biology

Sports/Physical Education, Career and Technical Education, or Mexican-American Topics (students read literature, read/discuss current events, history, multitude of other topics related to Latin America)

Is grade placement of newcomers based on age or previous grade enrolled in the student's home country?

A number of factors are usually considered when determining grade placement for newcomers, and placement is usually handled for each student on a case-by-case basis. In upper elementary and middle school, students are usually placed in the grade corresponding to their age, regardless of the students' prior grade level or academic experience in their home country. Benefits of the practice of placement by age:

- Avoids students "aging out" before they can complete graduation requirements

- Avoids overwhelming students who will be much older than their peers (e.g., 18-year-old freshmen), which increases the chances of students dropping out

In some cases, students may be placed in higher grades than their corresponding age, as was the case with Karina (see p. 63) because she had completed previous grades in her home country. The practice of placement based on previous educational experience may impact students in several ways:

- Requiring them to balance more rigorous coursework in higher grades, despite an initial lack of English proficiency

- Enabling them to progress faster through required high school courses and move toward graduation

In high school, grade placement is usually based on prior credits earned in the student's home country. This usually results in a student with a mixed schedule of courses from multiple grade levels. For example, a student may have the appropriate number of credits from his home country to be granted 11th grade status in the United States, but will end up taking some freshmen courses as well. Some students do not have transcripts or any other records from their home countries. In these cases, these students, regardless of age, are usually placed in freshmen courses. This poses an additional challenge for older students who could potentially age out before completing graduation requirements. Many districts offer these students other opportunities to complete coursework and acquire credits in an abbreviated amount of time.

What are some approaches for reviewing transcripts and granting credits?

Much like scheduling, the process of evaluating newcomers' transcripts and granting them high school credit for courses completed in their home countries varies widely. There is not one correct procedure. Nikki Lewis, Compliance Monitoring Department Coordinator, described the process as "very fluid and dynamic, taking a great deal of professional judgement and detective work." Joanna Rowley (BE/ESL director) said of transcript evaluation, "there is nothing straightforward about it. It's a very chaotic process and a guessing game sometimes, but it's something you get better at as you go."

Initial steps for beginning this process:

- Translate any available document(s), including transcripts and/or report cards
- Gather information about school of origin (you may find information online)
- Compare completed courses on the transcript to state-approved equivalents in order to grant appropriate credits

Please note that there is not one correct procedure. Be flexible. Here are further suggestions based on our observations, research, and interviews with educators working with and charged with grade placement of newcomers:

- Review transcripts on a case-by-case basis
- Pool your resources—personnel, documents, websites (such as for the school in the home country, which may provide general information on curriculum), and anything you can find and use to help you with this process

- Reach out to community members for translation assistance and for knowledge on schooling in other countries. For example, when Joanna Rowley in Midland ISD contacted Nigerians in the local community for help, she discovered that Nigerian schools were either English-based or French-based, which helped in determining student language abilities and possibly awarding LOTE (Languages other than English) credit.

- If you can locate phone numbers for the schools in the home country, attempt to call and speak with someone. You may need to use an interpreter, but this could be a critical step, especially if the student has no transcript or other paperwork. Having a conversation with someone can be very useful and quickly clear up any concerns or questions.

- Know that it can be a long process. Be willing to do the footwork, make the calls, and do the research. It may take a week or more to complete an evaluation.

Examples of transcript evaluation resources found online:

- *Evaluating Foreign Transcripts: The A-Z Manual*
  http://www.uft.org/files/attachments/evaluating-foreign-transcripts.pdf

- *Evaluating Foreign Transcripts: A Resource Guide for School Districts Provided by the Rhode Island Department of Education*
  http://www.ride.ri.gov/Portals/0/Uploads/Documents/Instruction-and-Assessment-World-Class-Standards/Instructional-Resources/Foreign-Transcript-Review/Foreign-Transcripts-Review-Resource-Guide-2-27-2012.pdf

UPON ENTERING HIGH SCHOOL, KARINA HAD THE OPPORTUNITY TO GAIN HER FOREIGN language credits by passing the level I and level II Spanish credits-by-exams, meaning she did not have to take any additional language courses to meet graduation requirements. She also took and passed the Advanced Placement Spanish exam and received a semester of college credit, as well. This helped Karina manage the setback of having to repeat the ninth grade and graduating a year later than she would have had she stayed in Mexico.

What credits are typically granted?

Credits are mostly awarded on a case-by-case basis.

- Credits for courses in math, science, PE, fine arts, and other electives that have course equivalents will usually be granted

- LOTE credit for the student's home language course(s) taken
  For example, if a Vietnamese student has two years of Vietnamese (equivalent to our ELA), some schools grant this as two years of LOTE.

  Students may also receive LOTE credit with successful results on foreign language CBEs (credit by exams) or other language proficiency/placement tests.

The following course credits are not typically granted:

- English
  English on a foreign transcript is most often English as a foreign language (EFL, equivalent to a LOTE course in the United States) and not the same curriculum as an English language arts class.

- World History and World Geography
  This is based on cultural differences and emphasis on various events. State standards and Common Core standards frame world events through the lens of the United States.

  Some districts offer an elective/local credit for these courses.

What do I do about missing or incomplete transcripts?

When a student arrives with no documentation of past coursework and no transcript, we must legally enroll the student no matter what (see enrollment procedures on p. 19). Similar to the guidance given regarding awarded credit with documentation, be flexible and willing to accept different types of documentation or evidence of completed coursework other than an official transcript. If possible, call the school in the home country to inquire about the student's history. With parental permission, the school may be able to give you the necessary information over the phone or via fax or email. Exhaust all possible sources of paperwork and documentation from parents or guardians and/or the school of origin. The following sentiment was echoed by the majority of school districts from my research: Err on the side of believing the student, in addition to accepting any documentation they may come with. The goal is to give as much credit as possible.

What can I do for an older newcomer who has few or no credits?

As previously mentioned, when a student arrives with no transcript or records of any kind, these students, regardless of age, are usually placed in freshmen courses. Additionally, some students arrive with a few credits but not enough to place them at grade level with their same-age peers. Many districts, however, offer a number of credit recovery opportunities for students to complete coursework and acquire credits in an abbreviated amount of time. Please note that many of these options are only offered after the students have been in the United States for several months to a year or more. This is to ensure that the students' language proficiency has progressed enough for them to be successful in a course where the instructor may not be sufficiently trained in sheltered instruction or SLA.

- CBE for LOTE for the student's home language
- CBE for other courses at student's request and/or for questionable credits (i.e., a student says he has completed Algebra I but has no records)
- After-school/evening/Saturday/night school
- Summer school
- Computer-based/online learning

Establishing a Newcomer Center, Program, or Team

What is a newcomer program, and how does it differ from other ELL programs?

Newcomer programs are specialized academic environments that serve newly arrive, immigrant ELLs for a limited period of time and are designed to provide guidance for students acculturating to the United States and to the U.S. school system. Programs specific to newcomers may differ from other language support programs (ESL or bilingual) in a number of ways.

Language Instruction: First, they typically only serve ELLs at the beginning levels of English proficiency and who are new to the country. From an instructional standpoint, newcomer programs have a stronger focus on language and literacy development, and more explicit instruction is provided for both social and academic English. The time afforded in a specialized newcomer class setting can ensure that more intense instruction is available to assist students in acquiring English skills. Successful newcomer teachers incorporate principles from ESL, sheltered instruction, and bilingual education research for determining appropriate curriculum, instructional methods, and formative/summative assessments. For core content areas, instruction is heavily accommodated and scaffolded to ensure comprehension.

Logistics: Newcomer programs take into account the flexible scheduling of courses that integrate extended time for instructional support. They also offer students opportunities to gain credit in an abbreviated amount of time. Related to the idea of successful outcomes for students, thoughtful staffing choices are made to ensure that educators with a heart for culturally responsive teaching are placed in newcomer programs. These individuals often receive sustainable, targeted professional development with teaching tools and strategies to further develop their craft. Time is also set aside for collaborative/team meetings and professional learning communities (PLCs) to develop curricula, draft assessments, examine student data, share instructional practices, and discuss students' needs. Effective processes are established to successfully transition students out of the newcomer program and into mainstream instruction, where further support can be offered through ESL services.

What are the options for newcomer programs?

Many factors play a role in establishing an effective newcomer program. Secondary newcomers in a single district or school may speak different home languages, come from different countries of origin, have different levels of literacy in English and/or their home language, and possess different levels of academic background knowledge. An effective newcomer program must balance available resources with the varying needs of the diverse newcomer population. There are likely countless variations to newcomer programming, but most can be categorized into one of three basic program models: programs within a school, separate-site programs, and whole-school programs (Short & Boyson, 2012). The following table summarizes each program model and characterizes some possible advantages and concerns.

TABLE 5.1 Options for Newcomer Programming

	Description	Advantages	Challenges
Programs within a school	Include partial- to full-day newcomer instruction at a mainstream school Might bus students from other campuses if each school does not have a newcomer program	Provide opportunities for newcomers to interact with the mainstream students for part of the day Provide greater access to support services Ease transition when exiting the newcomer program (for students who remain at the school) Offer greater course options	Require students zoned to a different "home" campus, upon exiting the newcomer program, to transition to a new school May limit the number of students who can participate based on available resources
Separate-site programs	House newcomers from multiple home campuses at a separate facility Offer full-day or half-day newcomer instruction (students then return to the home campus for the remainder of the day)	Can combine limited resources in one location Can plan schedules and other logistics around the needs of the newcomers	Often isolate newcomer students from the main student body, if only full-day programs are offered Lack native English-speaking role models (peers), if only full-day programs are offered May offer limited course offerings, sports, and electives May need extra transportation to bus students to centralized location
Whole-school programs	Are separate, self-contained schools for ongoing, comprehensive newcomer support Serve students who typically remain until they are promoted to high school or graduate, regardless of their language proficiency (i.e., students do not transition to another school)	Mirror resources and opportunities available for students at a mainstream middle, junior high, or high school Can connect students and families to outside services that may aid in their transition to the United States (medical, social, legal aid, etc.)	Isolate newcomers/ELLs from mainstream students Lack native English-speaking role models for peer interaction May offer limited course offerings, sports, and electives Need extra transportation to bus students to centralized location Are more expensive to run due to staffing, space, and resource requirements

How long should newcomers be supported in a separate-site program?

Most separate-site programs enroll students for a limited period of time before transitioning them to the regular language-support program (ESL/sheltered classes). The length of time in a program varies according to the program itself and can range from a few months to a year or two. Criteria for transiting vary by district and generally include such factors as student's date of entry into the program (e.g., at the beginning of the school year or midyear), educational background, score or proficiency level on reading, language, and literacy tests, and teacher recommendations.

What are some best practices to effectively transition students from a newcomer program?

Transition logistics:

- Establish transition teams and conduct transition meetings between the newcomer program staff and the receiving staff to discuss the students' needs.

- For students in a separate-site program, arrange and accompany the students on a site visit to their home school.

- Have each newcomer shadow a former newcomer.

- Schedule transitioning newcomers in the same class or with the same teacher.

Instructional support:

- Provide appropriate and ongoing staff development to all mainstream teachers who will be supporting newcomers once they leave the newcomer program.

- Ensure systematic and frequent monitoring and support of students.

- Assign teaching assistants to mainstream or sheltered classes.

How should resources be allocated to promote newcomer achievement?

Research over the last decade has uncovered a frequent discrepancy between the distribution of immigrant ELLs in various grade levels and funding and resource allocation for language support. For example, immigrant students and recently arrived immigrant students represent a larger percentage of the high school population than of the elementary population. However, funding of language acquisition programs tends to be highest in the elementary schools. In addition, a significantly smaller percentage of middle school and high school ELLs receive some kind of additional language support via ESL or sheltered instruction methods than ELLs in elementary settings (Capps et al., 2005; Ruiz-de-Velasco., 2000). These discrepancies are contrary to research that has asserted that recently arrived secondary ELLs frequently require substantial supplementary language support and additional services (Lee & Avitia, 2008). School district leadership is encouraged to address funding and resource allocation issues to ensure that more money is allotted to the secondary ELL programs, where the need is greatest. Doing so can ensure that newcomers can better acclimate to a school environment with properly trained, culturally responsive teachers who have the knowledge and resources to meet the cognitive, affective, and linguistic needs of their students.

Why is high-quality staff development essential for teachers of newcomers?

Teacher quality has a direct effect on developing academic literacy and content knowledge in ELLs, and this quality is related to teacher preparation. Researchers have asserted that the inadequate ability of school staff to instruct ELLs is a major challenge in overcoming the achievement gap (August & Shanahan, 2006; Crouch, 2012; Short & Echevarria, 2005; Ruiz-de-Velasco et al., 2000). At the foundation of a successful English-language development program are highly qualified teachers who are supported by research-based, sustainable professional development.

Despite the research regarding teacher quality and preparation, Short & Echevarria, (2005) described the disparity that often exists between students' needs and teachers' preservice and in-service development. This disparity results in a shortage of teachers appropriately trained to teach students with limited to no English proficiency. Furthermore, states may or may not require teachers to have additional credentials beyond basic certification to teach ELLs.

Thus, highly qualified teachers often have significant knowledge in the content but frequently lack an equal knowledge of second language acquisition or ESL methodology. Additionally, preservice and in-service trainings that exist for ELL instructional methods are often ineffective and brief.

Researchers have agreed that, in order for staff development to be effective in preparing teachers to appropriately educate ELLs, it should be continuous and intensive, with several opportunities for modeling, coaching, collaboration, and reflection (August & Shanahan, 2006; Lee & Avitia, 2008; Short & Echevarria, 2005). Providing considerable opportunities for professional development, including specialized trainings specific to ELLs, has resulted in improved classroom practices and increased student achievement.

Appendix A

Refugee Resettlement Agencies

Catholic Charities

https://catholiccharitiesusa.org/efforts/immigration-refugee-services

Church World Service (CWS)

http://www.cwsglobal.org/

Episcopal Migration Ministries (EMM)

http://www.episcopalchurch.org/page/episcopal-migration-ministries

Ethiopian Community Development Council (ECDC)

http://www.ecdcus.org/

Hebrew Immigrant Aid Society (HIAS)

http://www.hias.org/

International Rescue Committee (IRC)

http://www.rescue.org/

Lutheran Immigration and Refugee Services (LIRS)

http://lirs.org/

U.S. Committee for Refugees and Immigrants (USCRI)

http://refugees.org/

U.S. Conference of Catholic Bishops (USCCB)

http://www.usccb.org/

World Relief Corporation (WR)

http://www.worldrelief.org/

Appendix B

Immigrant, Refugee, and Culture Resources for Educators

BBC Country Profiles

From the BBC News organization, this website provides full profiles for countries and their territories around the globe, including information on history, politics, and economic background. They also include audio and video clips from BBC archives.

http://news.bbc.co.uk/2/hi/country_profiles/default.stm

Bringing Refugee Youth and Children Services

This is a comprehensive site for information on refugees, including access to the BRYCS Clearinghouse, an online collection of thousands of resources related to refugee and immigrant children and families.

http://www.brycs.org/

Center for Applied Linguistics: Immigrant and Refugee Integration

This site contains numerous links to various refugee resources, including several videos and publications.

http://www.cal.org/areas-of-impact/immigrant-refugee-integration

Cultural Orientation Resource Center

On this site, you'll find student welcome videos, activities, and phrasebooks in 14 languages as well as comprehensive information about various refugee and immigrant populations and more.

http://www.culturalorientation.net/

KidsHealth in the Classroom

This site offers a variety of free health resources, including teacher's guides, discussion questions, classroom activities and extensions, and printable handouts that will be useful when helping students' manage stress.

http://classroom.kidshealth.org/

National Child Traumatic Stress Network

This is a collection of helpful resources related to the mental health needs of refugee children and families.

http://www.nctsnet.org/

Office of Refugee Resettlement, U.S. Department of Health and Human Services

Here, you'll find general refugee information and resources, including downloadable/printable fact sheets on a variety of topics.

http://www.acf.hhs.gov/

Office of the United Nations High Commissioner for Refugees

This site of the U.N. agency responsible for leading and coordinating international action and protection for refugees worldwide has comprehensive information on refugees, including refugee-themed lesson modules in various subject areas for three different age groups.

http://www.unhcr.org/

The Refugee Experience

This grassroots, community-based organization is dedicated to recognizing and supporting refugees.

https://sites.google.com/site/therefugeeexperienceseries/home

Teaching Refugees with Limited Formal Schooling

Resources on this site include sample teaching units, tips for teachers, student and teacher videos, and more.

http://teachingrefugees.com/

Welcoming Refugees

Working via a cooperative agreement with the Office of Refugee Resettlement, this site provides a resource library, links to webinars, various articles, and many more refugee support resources.

http://www.welcomingrefugees.org/

Appendix C

List of Recommended Videos and Books

The following list has been compiled over the course of my years in education. These titles represent an array of books (at various reading levels), movies, and documentaries associated with ELLs, immigrant ELLs, refugees and/or their culture, and general cultural awareness and responsiveness. The books are categorized by cultural or geographical regions. I've found all of these titles to be interesting and informative, and I hope you will, too.

Documentaries

The Assaulted Dreams (2006)
Uli Stelzner

The Beast (2010)
Pedro Ultreras

Borderland (multi-part series) (2014)
Ivan O'Mahoney

Crossing Arizona (2006)
Dan DeVivo and Joseph Mathew

De Nadie (2005)
Tin Dirdamal

Farmingville (2004)
Carlos Sandoval and Catherine Tambini

La Voz Del Pueblo (2015)
Javier Montes

Last Train Home (2009)
Lixin Fan

Los Que Se Quedan (Those Who Remain) (2008)
Carlos Hagerman and Juan Carlos Rulfo

Lost Boys of Sudan (2004)
Megan Mylan and Jon Shenk

Maria in No Man's Land (Spanish with English Subtitles) (2011)
Marcela Zamora

Morristown (2007)
Anne Lewis

A Recycled Life (2006)
Leslie Iwerks

The Wall (2010)
Ricardo Martinez

Welcome to Shelbyville (2011)
Kim Snyder

Wetback: The Undocumented Documentary (2005)
Arturo Perez Torres

Which Way Home (2009)
Rebecca Cammisa

Movies

Babel (2006)
Alejandro González Iñárritu

A Better Life (2011)
Chris Weitz

Crash (2004)
Paul Haggis

Frozen River (2008)
Courtney Hunt

The Good Lie (2014)
Philippe Falardeau

Gran Torino (2008)
Clint Eastwood

McFarland, USA (2015)
Niki Caro

Outsourced (2006)
John Jeffcoat and George Wing

Sayonara (1957)
Paul Osborn

Sin Nombre (2009)
Cary Joji Fukunaga

Spare Parts (2015)
Sean McNamara

Stand and Deliver (1988)
Ramón Menéndez

Under the Same Moon (2007)
Patricia Riggen

Books
General Culture and Language

As Long as I Have My Own Bathroom: My Travel Adventures (2016)
Heather Jonasson

Disposable People? The Plight of Refugees (1993)
Judy A. Mayotte

From Every End of This Earth: 13 Families and the New Lives They Made in America (2009)
Steven V. Roberts

Hungry Planet: What the World Eats (2005)
Peter Menzel, Faith D'Aluisio, and Marion Nestle

I'm New Here (2015)
Anne Sibley O'Brien

Life in the Land of the Ice and Snow: Essays, Observations, and Lies (2014)
Heather Jonasson

Material World: A Global Family Portrait (1995)
Peter Menzel and Charles C. Mann

The Mother Tongue: English and How It Got That Way (2001)
Bill Bryson

Mother Tongue: My Family's Globe-Trotting Quest to Dream in Mandarin, Laugh in Arabic, and Sing in Spanish (2016)

Christine Gilbert

The New Kids: Big Dreams and Brave Journeys at a High School for Immigrant Teens (2012)

Brooke Hauser

Outcasts United: An American Town, a Refugee Team, and One Woman's Quest to Make a Difference (2009)

Warren St. John

Swimming to America (2005)

Alice Mead

We Can't Teach What We Don't Know (2006)

Gary R. Howard

Where Children Sleep (2010)

James Mollison

By Region

Africa

Brothers in Hope: The Story of the Lost Boys of Sudan (2007)

Mary Williams

The Color of Home (2012)

Mary Hoffman

Echoes of the Lost Boys of Sudan (2011)

James Disco and Susan Clark

Home of the Brave (2008)

Katherine Applegate

A Long Walk to Water (2011)

Linda Sue Park

The Lost Boys of Sudan (2012)

Jeff Burlingame

The Lost Boys of Sudan: An American Story of the Refugee Experience (2006)

Mark Bixler

My Name Is Sangoel (2009)

Karen Williams and Khadra Mohammed

My Two Blankets (2015)

Irena Kobald

The Red Pencil (2014)

Andrea Pinkney

Tears of the Desert: A Memoir of Survival in Darfur (2008)

Halima Bashir and Damien Lewis

Teenage Refugees from Rwanda Speak Out (1997)

Aimable Twagilimana

They Poured Fire on Us from the Sky: The True Story of Three Lost Boys from Sudan (2015)

Benjamin Ajak, Benson Deng, Alephonsion Deng, and Judy A. Bernstein

What is the What: The Autobiography of Valentino Achak Deng (2006)

Dave Eggers

When I Get Older: The Story behind "Wavin' Flag" (2012)

K'NAAN and Sol Sol

Asia

All the Broken Pieces (2009)

Ann E. Burg

Bamboo People (2012)

Mitali Perkins

Children of the River (1991)

Linda Crew

Dia's Story Cloth: The Hmong People's Journey to Freedom (1998)

Dia Cha

Escape from Saigon: How a Vietnam War Orphan Became an American Boy (2008)

Andrea Warren

First They Killed My Father: A Daughter of Cambodia Remembers (2006)

Loung Ung

In the Shadow of the Banyan: A Novel (2012)

Vaddey Ratner

Inside Out and Back Again (2011)

Thanhha Lai

Letters from Burma (2010)

Aung San Suu Kyi

Mai Ya's Long Journey (2005)

Sheila Cohen

My Freedom Trip (1998)

Frances Park and Ginger Park

A Song for Cambodia (2008)

Michelle Lord

The Spirit Catches You and You Fall Down: A Hmong Child, Her American Doctors, and the Collision of Two Cultures (2012)

Anne Fadiman

The Stone Goddess (2005)

Minfong Ho

Tangled Threads (2003)
Pegi Deitz Shea

Weeping Under This Same Moon (2008)
Jana Laiz

When Broken Glass Floats: Growing Up Under the Khmer Rouge (2001)
Chanrithy Him

The Whispering Cloth (1996)
Pegi Shea and Anita Riggio

Caribbean

90 Miles to Havana (2012)
Enrique Flores-Galbis

How Many Days to America? A Thanksgiving Story (1990)
Eve Bunting

Mama's Nightingale: A Story of Immigration and Separation (2015)
Edwidge Danticat

Serafina's Promise (2015)
Ann E. Burg

Europe

Adem's Cross (1996)
Alice Mead

The Blessing Cup (2013)
Patricia Polacco

The Cat from Kosovo (2001)
Mary Jane Hampton

Day of the Pelican (2010)
Katherine Paterson

Fiona's Lace (2014)
Patricia Polacco

Girl of Kosovo (2011)
Alice Mead

How I Learned Geography (2008)
Uri Shulevitz

The Keeping Quilt, 25th Anniversary Edition (2013)
Patricia Polacco

The Memory Coat (1999)
Elvira Woodruff

Something about America (2007)
Maria Testa

Zlata's Diary: A Child's Life in Wartime Sarajevo (2006)
Zlata Filipovic

Latin America

Enrique's Journey (2014)
Sonia Nazario

The House on Mango Street (1991)
Sandra Cisneros

I Lived on Butterfly Hill (2015)
Marjorie Agosín

Red Midnight (2003)
Ben Mikaelsen

The Secret Story of Sonia Rodriguez (2010)
Alan Lawrence Sitomer

Middle East

The Breadwinner Trilogy (2009)
Deborah Ellis

Children of War: Voices of Iraqi Refugees (2010)
Deborah Ellis

Four Feet, Two Sandals (2007)
Karen Lynn Williams and Khadra Mohammad

Out of Iraq: Refugees' Stories in Words, Paintings, and Music (2010)
Sybella Wilkes

Playing War (2005)
Kathy Beckwith

Shooting Kabul (2011)
N. H. Senzai

Under the Persimmon Tree (2008)
Suzanne Fisher Staples

Words in the Dust (2013)
Trent Reedy

Ziba Came on a Boat (2007)
Liz Lofthouse

Appendix D

ELL/Newcomer Instructional Resources

The following list represents a sampling of the instructional resources educators are currently using to meet the needs of ELLs/newcomers. This list has been compiled from classroom and school visits, interviews, and my ongoing research. It contains books for teachers, language development programs, websites, leveled reader collections for students, and publishing companies and is organized by subject.

General Classroom Resources

Colorín Colorado

A wide range of research-based information, activities, and advice, including ELL resources by state

http://www.colorincolorado.org

Interactive Notebooks and English Language Learners (2009)

Marcia Carter, Anita Hernandez, and Jeannine Richison

News in Levels: World News for Students of English

http://www.newsinlevels.com

Notebook Foldables for Spirals, Binders, and Composition Books (2009)

Dinah Zike

Oxford English Language Picture Dictionary

Oxford University Press

Content Area Resources

Oxford Picture Dictionary in the Content Areas

Oxford University Press

ACCESS American History
ACCESS English Language Arts
ACCESS Math
ACCESS Science
ACCESS World History

Great Source/Houghton Mifflin Harcourt

FAST Math

Intervention program designed for ELLs that are two or more years behind in math and have limited or interrupted formal schooling; developed by Fairfax County, VA

http://www.ncela.us/files/uploads/15/Fastmath1of10.pdf

Language Learning and Reading Programs

ACCESS Newcomers

Great Source/Houghton Mifflin Harcourt

Champion of Ideas

Ballard & Tighe Publishing

Edge Fundamentals

National Geographic School Publishing

Finish Line for ELLs: English Proficiency Practice
Continental Press

Grammar Sense Series
Oxford University Press

Inside Phonics
National Geographic School Publishing

Inside the U.S.A.
National Geographic School Publishing

Keys to Learning
Pearson Longman

Reading Basics
Reading Expeditions
National Geographic School Publishing

Reading Street
Scott Foresman

RIGOR (Reading Instructional Goals for Older Readers) (Intervention Program)
Benchmark Education

Readers and Book Sets (by publisher)

High Noon Books
Comprehensive inventory of titles including Hi/Lo readers, high interest fiction and non-fiction, classics, graphic novels, and minimal-text books

Saddleback Educational Publishing
Wide array of Hi/Lo readers and leveled collections, including classics and Shakespeare as well as:
ELL Teen Literacy Library
Newcomers in Action
Welcome Newcomers Library

Software Programs
ELLIS
Pearson

ESL ReadingSmart
Edmentum

System 44
Houghton Mifflin Harcourt

Appendix E

List of Latin and Greek Morphemes

Prefixes		
a, ab	away, from, apart, away from	avert, astringent, abnormal, abstain, ablation, abduct, abscission
a, an	not, without	asymmetrical, amoral, anachronism
ad	to, toward	adhesion, adjoin
ambi, amphi	both	amphitheater, ambiguous, ambivalent
ante	before	antecedent, anterior, anteroom
anti	against	antiaircraft, antipathy, anticlimax
bene	good	benevolence, beneficent, benefit, benevolent
circum	around, round, surrounding	circumstance, circumference, circumscribe, circumnavigate
con, com, co	together, with	continue, communal, connection, cooperation, company
contra, counter	against, opposed to	contraindicate, contradiction, countermeasure, counterplot, counterpoint
de	down from, away from, reverse	departure, derailment, demerit, debrief
dia	through	dialectic, dialogue, diagnosis, diameter, diagonal
dis	opposite of, away	disinherit, disperse, disenfranchise, dismissal
dys	ill, bad, impaired, difficult	dysplasia, dysfunctional, dyslexia
epi	upon, above	epidemic, epigram, epitaph, epicenter, epidermis, epilogue
ex	out, out of, away from, formerly	exoskeleton, exotic, exterior, exit, exclusion
fore	in front	forehead, forecast, foreshadow, foreclose, forebode, forearm
hyper	over, above, beyond, excessively	hyperactive, hypersensitive, hypersonic, hyperventilate
hypo	under, beneath, below	hypochondriac, hypothermia, hypodermic, hypodermal
il	not	illiterate, illegal, illogical, illusion
in	in, into, within	incision, insertion, inclusion
in	not	incredible, inhospitable, infinite, infinitesimal, incapable
inter	between, among	interact, interpret, intervene, intercept, interstate

Prefixes

intra, intro	within	intramurals, intravenous, introduction, introspection
luc	light	lucent, lucid, translucent
mega	large, great	megawatt, megahertz, megaphone, megabyte
mis	wrong(ly), incorrect(ly)	misunderstood, mistake, misspell, misprint, miscalculate
multi	many	multisyllabic, multicolored, multiply, multitude, multivitamin
neo	new	neophyte, Neolithic, neonatal, neoplasm
non	not	nonentity, nonpayment, nonprofessional, noninvasive, nonsense
nov	new	novel, novelist, novelty, novice
omni	all	omnipresent, omnipotent, omniscient
pan	all	pandemic, panacea, panorama, pantheism, panic
per	through, throughout, over, large, high	perceive, perfuse, pervade, pervasive, perfect
peri	around	peritoneum, periscope, perimeter
poly	many	polygon, polygamy, polyester, polyethylene, polyglot, polytechnic, polysyllabic
post	after	postpone, postscript, postoperative, postnasal, postpartum, post-war
pre	before	preview, premier, premium, preface, prewar
prim	first	primer, prime, primary, primitive
pro	in favor of, forward, in place of	probiotics, project, projectile, pronoun
proto	first	protoplasm, prototype, protocol, proton
re	back, again	repetitive, retraction, revert, repetition, retrace, refurbish, regenerate
retro	back, backward	retrospect, retroactive, retrograde, retrorocket
se	away, apart	segregation, seclusion, secession, sequester
sub	under, below	subterfuge, submarine, subterranean
super	over, above, beyond	superfluous, supervisory
sym, syn	together, with	symbiotic, symphony, symmetry, symbol, symptom, synthesis, synchronize, synonym, synonymous
trans	across, over	transport, transcend, transition, translate, transmission
ultra	excessively	ultramodern, ultrasound, ultralight, ultraviolet

Roots

acer, acr	sharp, bitter	acerbic, acid, acrid, acerbate
alter	other	alter ego, alternative, alternate
ambul	walk	ambulatory, ambulance, amble, somnambular
amor	love	amiable, enamored, amorous
annu, enni	ear	annual, annually, anniversary, biennial, centennial, perennial
anthropo	man	misanthrope, philanthropy, anthropology
aqua	water	aqueduct, aqueous, aquarium
arch	ruler, chief, first	archdiocese, archenemy, monarch, anarchy
aster	star	astronomy, asterisk, astronaut
aud, audit	hear, listen to	audiology, auditorium, audition, audience
bene	good	benefactor, benevolent, benign, benediction
bibl	book	bibliography, bibliophile, Bible
bio	life	biome, biometrics, biology, biography, biopic
calor	heat	caloric, calorie
cap	take, hold	capable, capture
capit, capt	head, chief, leader	captain, caption, capital, captor
cardi	heart	cardiovascular, cardiogram, cardiology, cardiac
carn	flesh	carnal, carnivorous, incarnate, reincarnation
caus, caut	burn	caustic, cauldron, cauterize, holocaust
cause, cuse ,cus	cause, motive	excuse, accusation, because, cause
cede, cess	move, yield	procedure, concede, recede, precede, accede, success
chrom	color	chromosome, polychrome, chromatic
chron	time	chronology, synchronize, chronicle, chronological
clud	shut	conclude, include, exclude
corp, corpor	body	corporation, corpse, corporal

Roots

crat, cracy	power, rule	democrat, aristocrat, democracy, theocracy
cred	believe	credit, credible, incredible, credo
crux, cruc	cross	crucify, crucifix, crucial, crucible, crux
crypt	secret, hidden	crypt, cryptic, cryptogram
culpa	blame	culprit, culpable
cur, curs	run, course	concurrent, current, incur, occur, precursor, cursive, cursor
dem	people	epidemic, democracy, demography
derm	skin	hypodermic, dermatology, epidermis, taxidermy
deus	god	deity, deify
dic(t)	tell, speak	dictum, dictionary, dictation, dictate, dictator, edict, contradict, benediction
dorm	sleep	dormitory, dormancy, dormant
dox	belief	doxology, paradox, orthodox
duc(t)	lead	seduce, produce, reduce, induce, introduce, conduct
dyna	power	dynamite, hydrodynamics, dynamic, dynasty
equ	equal	equitable, equinox, equilibrium, equivalent
fac	make, do	manufacture, fact, factory
fer	bear, carry	fertile, ferry, transfer, refer, infer, defer, aquifer
fid	faith, trust	fidelity, confederate, confidence, infidelity, infidel, federal
flu, flux	flowing	influenza, influence, fluid, flush, confluence, fluently, fluctuate
fort	strong	fortress, fortitude, fort, fortify
fract	break	refract, infraction, fracture
frater	brother	fraternity, fraternal, fraternize
gen	race, birth, kind	generate, genetic, eugenics, genesis, genealogy, generation, antigen
geo	earth	geometry, geography, geocentric, geology, geothermal
greg	flock, herd	congregation, congregate, gregarious

Roots

gress	go	progress, progression, egress
gyn	woman	gynecology, gynecologist
hetero	different	heterogeneous, heteromorphic, heteronym
homo, homeo	same	homogenize, homogeneous, homonym, homeostasis
homo	man	homage, Homo sapiens
hydr	water	hydrate, dehydrate, hydrant, hydraulic, hydrogen, hydrophobia
jac, jec	throw	projectile, projector, eject
lact	milk	lactose, lactate
junct	join	juncture, junction, adjunct, conjunction
lat	side	lateral, equilateral, unilateral
laud	praise	applause, laudable, plausible, applaud
lect	gather, choose, read	collection, lecture, election, electorate
leg, legis	law	legislate, legal, legislature, legitimize
lith	stone	monolithic, megalith, batholith, Neolithic
locu, loqu	speak	eloquent, loquacious, colloquial, circumlocution, elocution
log, logy	speech, word, study of	catalogue, dialogue, prologue, psychology, logical, zoology
magn(i)	large, great	magnificent, manufacture, magnate, magnitude, magnum
mal	bad, evil	malnourished, malignant, malicious, malfunction, malcontent,
man, manu	hand	manual, manicure, manacle, maneuver, emancipate, manufacture
meter, metr	measure	meter, barometer, thermometer, symmetry
micro	small	microscope, microwave, micrometer, microbe
mit, miss	send	emit, remit, commit, submit, permit, transmit, mission, permission, missile
mob, mov, mot	move	motor, movie, motivate, emotional, mobile, movie, motivation, emote, immortal
mute	change	mutate, mutation, immutable
nasc, nat	birth, spring forth	nascent, innate, natal, native, renaissance, nativity

Roots		
nihil, nil	nothing	annihilate
noct	night	nocturnal
nym	name	antonym, synonym, acronym, pseudonym, homonym, anonymous
oner, onus	burden	onerous, onus
ortho	straight, right, correct	orthopedic, orthodontist, unorthodox, orthodox
pac	peace	Pacific Ocean, pacify, pacifier, pacifist
path	feeling, disease	telepathy, sympathy, antipathy, apathy, pathos
pecc	fault, sin	impeccable, peccadilloes
ped, pod	foot	pedal, pedestrian, impede, centipede, tripod, podiatry, podium
pel, puls	urge, drive	compel, impel, expel, repel, propel, pulse, impulse, pulsate, compulsory, repulsive
pend, pen	hang	pendulum, pendant, suspend, appendage, pensive, impending
phil	love	philanthropist, philosophy
phob	fear	claustrophobia, agoraphobia, homophobia, arachnophobia
phon	sound	phonograph, telephone, homophone, euphonious, phonetic
photo	light	photographic, photogenic, photosynthesis
physio	nature	physiological, physiology
plac	please, appease	placebo, placid, placate, complacent
plen, plete	fill	complete, replenish, plentiful, deplete
pli, plic, plex	fold, bend	complicate, pliable, multiplication
polis	city	metropolis, police, megalopolis, politics, acropolis, Indianapolis
pon, pos	place, put	component, postpone, component, position, deposit, proponent
popul	people	population, populous, popular
port	carry	transport, import, export, support, report, portfolio

Roots

prec-i	price	precious, depreciate, appreciate
prim	first, early	primal, primary, primitive, primeval
pseudo	false	pseudonym, pseudoscience
psych	mind	psychiatry, psyche, psychology, psychosis
pulmo	lung	pulmonary
pung, punct	point	pungent, punctual, puncture
quasi	like, but not really	quasi-scientific, quasi-official, quasi-war, quasi-corporation
sanct	holy	sanctuary, sanctimonious, sanction
scien	know, knowledge	science, conscience, omniscient
scope	sight	microscope, telescope, kaleidoscope, periscope, stethoscope
scrib, script	write	scribe, scribble, inscribe, describe, subscribe, script, manuscript
sequ, secut	follow	consequence, sequence, sequel, consecutive
sol	alone	solstice, solo, solitary, solitude, solitaire
solv, solut	loosen	solvent, solve, solution, absolve, resolution, resolute, resolve
somn	sleep	somnambulant, somnolent, somniferous
son	sound	resonance, resonate, sonic, unison
soph	wise	sophomore, philosopher, sophisticated
spec(t)	look	spectator, spectacle, aspect, inspect, speculate, respect, prospect, retrospective, expect
spir	breath, breathe	respirator, aspire, expire, perspire, conspire
string, strict	tighten	stringent, astringent, stricture, strict, restriction, constrict
stru, struct	build	construct, instruct, destruction, structure
tang, tact, tig	touch	tangible, intangible, tactile, contact, contiguous
tele	far, far off	teleport, television, telephone, telegram, telescope, telephoto, telecast, telepathy
tend, tens	hold	contend, pretend, intend, superintendent, tendency, tension
terra	earth	terrarium, territory, terrain, terrestrial, extraterrestrial, terra firma

Roots

theo	god	theology, atheism, polytheism, monotheism
tom	cut	anatomy, atom, appendectomy, dichotomy, tonsillectomy, dichotomy
tort	twist	distortion, torture, retort, distort, contort, torturous
tract	draw, drag	retractable, attract, tractor, subtract, abstract, extract
ven(t)	come	ventricle, ventilate, vent, convention, venue, avenue, venture, event, advent, prevent
vert, vers	turn	convertible, controversial, avert, divert, invert, versatile, reversible
vid, vis	see	evidence, providence, video, provide, visual, vista, visit, vision
viv	live	survivor, vivacious, revive, vivid
voc	call, speak, voice	vocabulary, convocation, vocal, vocation, avocation

Latin and Greek Numbers

One	uni	union, unilateral, uniform, university, united
	mono	monotheism, monastic, monotone, monologue
Two	du(o)	duplication, duet, duplex,
	bi	biweekly, bilingual, bicycle, binomial
Three	tri	tricycle, triad, triangle, triceps, trichromatic, triplicate
Four	quad(ri) (ra)	quadruplets, quadruple, quadrangle, quadriceps, quadruped
	tetra	tetragonal, tetrahedron, tetrameter, tetrapod
Five	quin	quintuplet, quintet, quintessence
	pent(a)	pentameter, pentagon, Pentateuch, pentathlon, pentacle, Pentecost
Six	sex	sextant, sexagenarian, sextuplet, sextet
	hex(a)	hexagram, hexadecimal, hexachord, hexagon, hexameter
Seven	sept	septennial, septet, septuagenarian
	hept(a)	heptahedron, heptameter, heptagon
Eight	octo	octagon, octogenarian, octave, octet, octopus
Nine	non	nonagenarian, nonagon
Ten	dec	decagon, decahedron, decade, decalogue, decameter, decimal
One hundred	cent	centipede, centimeter, centennial, century
One thousand	mil, milli	milliliter, millimeter, millennium, millipede, milliliter, millisecond

Appendix F

Signal and Transition Words

DESCRIPTION/ LIST	SEQUENCE	COMPARISON/ CONTRAST	CAUSE AND EFFECT	PROBLEM/ SOLUTION
for example	first, second, third	however	because	
such as	in the first place	but	since	
to illustrate	first of all	as well as	therefore	
for instance	then	on the other hand	consequently	
in addition	before	while	as a consequence	
and	after	although	in order that	
again	last	different from	so that	
moreover	meanwhile	less than, fewer than	as a result	
also, too	now	also, too	then	
furthermore	finally	like	if...then	
another	for one thing	though	thus	
first of all	next	much as	due to	
second	subsequent (-ly)	yet	accordingly	
additionally	later	similarly	for this reason	
not only...but also		similar to		
		whereas		
		as opposed to		
		still		
		in contrast		

References

American Psychiatric Association. (2013). *Diagnostic and statistical manual of mental disorders* (5th ed.). Arlington, VA: American Psychiatric Publishing.

Arechiga, D. (2012). *Reaching English language learners in every classroom: Energizers for teaching and learning* (1st ed.). New York, NY: Routledge.

Asher, J. J. (1969). The total physical response approach to second language learning. *The Modern Language Journal, 53*(1), 3-17.

Aud, S., Fox, M., & KewalRamani, A. (2010). *Status and trends in the education of racial and ethnic groups* (NCES 2010-016). Retrieved from National Center for Education Statistics website: http://nces.ed.gov/pubs2010/2010015.pdf

August, D. & Shanahan, R. (Eds.). (2006). *Developing literacy in second-language minority learners: Report of the National Literacy Panel on Language Minority Children and Youth.* Mahwah, NJ: Erlbaum.

Breiseth, L. (2011). *A guide for engaging ELL families: Twenty strategies for school leaders.* Retrieved from http://www.color-incolorado.org/sites/default/files/Engaging_ELL_Families_FINAL.pdf

Brewster, C., & Railsback, J. (2017). *Building trust with schools and diverse families.* Retrieved from http://www.adlit.org/article/21522/

Buly, M. R. (2010). *English language learners in literacy workshops.* Urbana, IL: National Council of Teachers of English.

Bureau of Refugee and Immigrant Assistance. (n.d.) *Caring for refugee students: Guide for school nurses.* Retrieved from https://otda.ny.gov/programs/bria/documents/WtOS-School-Nurse-Brochure.pdf

Burt, M., Peyton, J. K., & Adams, R. (2003). *Reading and adult English language learners: A review of the research.* Washington, DC: Center for Applied Linguistics

Camarota, S. (2007). *Immigrants in the United States, 2007: A profile of America's foreign-born population.* Retrieved from Center for Immigration Studies website: http://www.cis.org/articles/2007/back1007.pdfCapps, R., Fix, M., Murray, J., Ost, J., Passel, J., & Herwantoro, S. (2005). *Immigration and the No Child Left Behind Act.* Retrieved from Urban Institute website: http://www.urban.org/publications/311230.html

Child Trends Data Bank. (2012). *Dropout rates.* Retrieved from http://www.childtrends-databank.org/pdf/1_PDF.pdf

Commins, N. (2012). How do English language learners learn content-area concepts through their second language? In E. Hamayan & R. Field (Eds.), *English language learners at school: A guide for administrators* (pp. 44–46). Philadelphia, PA: Caslon Publishing.

Concordia University. (2017). *How comfortable classrooms lead to a better student community.* Retrieved from https://education.cu-portland.edu/blog/news/welcoming-classrooms-better-students/

Cross, T., Bazron, B., Dennis, K., & Isaacs, M. (1989). *Towards a culturally competent system of care, volume 1 .* Washington, DC: CASSP Technical Assistance Center, Center for Child Health and Mental Health Policy, Georgetown University Child Development Center.

Crouch, D. (2016). *5 steps for effective home visits.* Retrieved from http://edu.stemjobs.com/home-visits/

Crouch, R. (2012). *The United States of education: The changing demographics of the United States and their schools.* Retrieved from http://www.centerforpubliceducation.org/You-May-Also-Be-Interested-In-landing-page-level/Organizing-a-School-YMABI/The-United-States-of-education-The-changing-demographics-of-the-United-States-and-their-schools.html

Cummins, J. (1979). Cognitive/academic language proficiency, linguistic interdependence, the optimum age question, and some other matters. *Working Papers on Bilingualism, 19*, 121–129.

Cummins, J. (1981). The role of primary language development in promoting educational success for language minority students. *Schooling and Language Minority Students: A Theoretical Framework* (pp. 30–49). Los Angeles, CA: California State Department of Education.

Dryden-Peterson, S. (2011). *Refugee education: A global review.* Retrieved from http://www.unhcr.org/4fe317589.pdf

Dryden-Peterson, S. (2015). *The educational experiences of refugee children in countries of first asylum.* Retrieved from https://www.migrationpolicy.org/research/educational-experiences-refugee-children-countries-first-asylum

Dutro, S., & Moran, C. (2003). Rethinking English language instruction: An architectural approach. In G. G. García (Ed.), *English learners: Reaching the highest level of English literacy* (pp. 227–258). Newark, DE: International Reading Association.

Echevarria, J., Vogt, M.E., & Short, D. (2017). *Making content comprehensible for English learners: The SIOP Model,* Fifth Edition.. New York, NY: Pearson.

Gándara, P. (2005). *Fragile futures: Risk and vulnerability among Latino high achievers.* Retrieved from Educational Testing Services website: http://www.ets.org/Media/Research/pdf/PICFRAGFUT.pdf

Goldenberg, C., & Coleman, R. (2010). *Promoting academic achievement among English learners: A guide to the research.* Thousand Oaks, CA: Corwin Press

Grieco, E., & Trevelyan, E. (2010). *Place of birth of the foreign-born population: 2009* (ACSBR 09-1509-15). Retrieved from United States Census Bureau website: http://www.census.gov/prod/2010pubs/acsbr09-15.pdf

Hanson, H., Bisht, B., & Motamedi, J. G. (2016). *Advanced course enrollment and performance among English learner students in Washington State.* (REL 2017–187). Washington, DC: U.S. Department of Education, Institute of Education Sciences, National Center for Education Evaluation and Regional Assistance, Regional Educational Laboratory Northwest. Retrieved from http://ies.ed.gov/ncee/edlabs

Haynes, J., & Zacarian, D. (2010). *Teaching English language learners: Across the content areas.* Alexandria, VA: ASCD.

Henyan, A. (2016). *Overcoming education challenges for refugee children.* Retrieved from http://www.borgenmagazine.com/education-challenges-refugee-children/

Johnson, M. L. (2013). *A phenomenological narrative study of the lived experiences of successful high school immigrants* (Doctoral dissertation). Beaumont, TX: Lamar University. Retrieved from https://search.proquest.com/openview/e6a3218e-05a5ea79303911de8a50fa9d/1?pq-origsite=gscholar&cbl=18750&diss=y

Kagan, S., & Kagan, M. (2009). *Kagan cooperative learning.* San Clemente, CA: Kagan Publishing.

Klein, E. (2016). *Decrease classroom clutter to increase creativity.* Retrieved from https://www.edutopia.org/blog/decrease-classroom-clutter-increase-creativity-erin-klein

Klopfenstein, K. (2004). The advanced placement expansion of the 1990s: How did traditionally underserved students fare? *Education Policy Analysis Archives, 12*(68). Retrieved from http://www.epaa.asu.edu

Krashen, S. (1981). *Second language acquisition and second language learning.* New York: Prentice-Hall.

Krebs, G. (2103). *An American education: refugees and new immigrants face challenges to graduation.* Retrieved from https://www.deseretnews.com/article/865570328/An-American-education-refugees-and-new-immigrants-face-challenges-to-graduation.html

Law, B., & Eckes, M. (2000). *The more-than-just-surviving handbook: ESL for every classroom teacher* (2nd ed.). Winnipeg: Portage & Main Press.

Learning Disabilities Association of America. (2017). *New to LD.* Retrieved from https://ldaamerica.org/support/new-to-ld/

Lee, M., & Avitia, D. (2008). *Getting it right: Ensuring a quality education for English-language learners in New York.* Retrieved from Education Week website: http://www.edweek.org/media/nyic_ellbrief_final.pdf

Legters, N., McDill, E., & McPartland, J. (1994). *Section II. Rising to the challenge: Emerging strategies for educating students at risk.* Washington D.C.: U.S. Department of Education, Office of Educational Statistics and Improvement. Retrieved from http://www2.ed.gov/pubs/EdReformStudies/EdReforms/chap6a.html

Lindsey, R., Nuri-Robins, K., & Terrell, R. (2009). *Cultural proficiency: A manual for school leaders.* Thousand Oaks, CA: Corwin.

Linsin, M. (2011). *How your classroom environment can improve behavior.* Retrieved from https://www.smartclassroommanagement.com/2011/10/08/classroom-environment/

Lopez, G., & Radford, J. (2015). *Facts on U.S. immigrants, 2015: Statistical portrait of the foreign-born population in the United States.* Retrieved from http://www.pewhispanic.org/2017/05/03/facts-on-u-s-immigrants/

Lyman, F. T. (1981). The responsive classroom discussion: the inclusion of all students. In A. Anderson (Ed.), *Mainstreaming digest* (pp. 109–113). College Park, MD: University of Maryland Press.

Marzano, R. (2004). *Building background knowledge for academic achievement: Research on what works in schools.* Alexandria, VA: ASCD.

Marzano, R., Pickering, D. J., & Pollock, J. E. (2001). *Classroom instruction that works.* Alexandria, VA: MCREL, ASCD.

Masten, A., & Narayan, A. (2012). Child development in the context of disaster, war, and terrorism: Pathways of risk and resilience. *The Annual Review of Psychology,* 227–257. doi 10.1146/annurev-psych-120710-100356

Moon, B., Hoffman, R., Novak, J. D., & Cañas, A. J. (Eds.). (2011). *Applied concept mapping: Capturing, analyzing, and organizing knowledge.* Boca Raton, FL: CRC Press.

Mossaad, N. (2016.) *Annual flow report, refugees and asylees: 2014.* Washington, DC: United States Department of Homeland Security, Office of Immigration Statistics. Retrieved from https://www.dhs.gov/sites/default/files/publications/Refugees_Asylees_2014.pdf

National Conference of State Legislatures. (2014). *Undocumented student tuition: state action.* Retrieved from http://www.ncsl.org/research/education/undocumented-student-tuition-state-action.aspx

Nessel, D., & Dixon, C.(Eds.). (2008). *Using the language experience approach with English language learners: Strategies for engaging students and developing literacy.* Thousand Oaks, CA: Corwin Press.

O'Malley, J., & Chamot, U. (1990). *Learning strategies in second language acquisition.* New York, NY: Cambridge University Press.

Ortega, L. (2009). *Understanding second language acquisition.* New York, NY: Hodder Education.

Payne, R. (2003). *A framework for understanding poverty* (3rd ed.). Highlands, TX: aha! Process, Inc.

Pedersen, P. (1994). *Five stages of culture shock: critical incidents around the world.* Westport, CT: Greenwood Publishing Group, Inc.

Pope, A. (2015). *Infographic: The screening process for refugee entry into the United States.* Retrieved from https://www.whitehouse.gov/blog/2015/11/20/infographic-screening-process-refugee-entry-united-states

Ruiz-de-Velasco, J., Fix, M., & Clewell, B. (2000). *Overlooked and underserved: Immigrant students in U.S. secondary schools.* Retrieved from Urban Institute website: http://www.urban.org/publications/310022.html#n6

Salva, C., & Matis, A. (2017). *Boosting achievement: Reaching students with interrupted or minimal education.* San Clemente, CA: Canter Press.

Sánchez, M. T., Parker, C., Akbayin, B., & McTigue, A. (2010). *Processes and challenges in identifying learning disabilities among students who are English language learners in three New York State districts* (Issues & Answers Report, REL 2010–No. 085). Washington, DC: U.S. Department of Education, Institute of Education Sciences, National Center for Education Evaluation and Regional Assistance, Regional Educational Laboratory Northeast and Islands. Retrieved from http://ies.ed.gov/ ncee/edlabs

Santa, C., Havens, L., & Valdes, B. (2004). *Project CRISS: Creating independence through student-owned strategies.* Dubuque, IA: Kendall/Hunt

Saunders, W., Goldenberg, C., & Marcelletti, D. (2013). English language development: Guidelines for instruction. *American Educator, 37*(2), 13–25, 38–39.

Seidlitz, J., Base, M., Lara, M., Rodríguez, M., & Hartill, M. (2014). *ELLs in Texas: What administrators need to know.* San Clemente, CA: Canter Press.

Seidlitz, J., Base, M., Lara, M., & Smith, H. (2016). *ELLs in Texas: What teachers need to know.* San Clemente, CA: Canter Press.

Seidlitz, J., Jones, C., & Motley, N. (2011). *The diverse learner flip book: A use-friendly guide for meeting the needs of all students.* San Clemente, CA: Canter Press.

Seidlitz, J., & Kenfield, K. (2011). *38 great academic language builders: Activities for math, science, social studies, language arts...and just about everything else.* San Clemente, CA: Canter Press.

Seidlitz J., & Perryman, B. (2011). *7 Steps to a language-rich interactive classroom: Research-based strategies for engaging all students.* San Clemente, CA: Canter Press.

Short, D. J., & Boyson, B. A. (2012). *Helping newcomer students succeed in secondary schools and beyond.* Washington, DC: Center for Applied Linguistics.

Short, D. & Echevarria, J. (2005) Teacher skills to support English-language learners. *Educational Leadership, 62*, 8-13. Retrieved from http://www.ascd.org

Smith, Z. (2016). *7 tips for successful home visits.* Retrieved from http://midtesol. org/7-tips-for-successful-home-visits/

Swanson, C. (2003). *Who graduates? Who doesn't? A statistical portrait of public high school graduation, class of 2001.* Retrieved from Urban Institute website: http://www.urban.org/UploadedPDF/410934_WhoGraduates.pdf

Taba, H. (1967). *Teachers' handbook for elementary social studies.* Reading, MA: Addison-Wesley.

Thornbury, A. (2010). *T is for translation.* Retrieved from http://scottthornbury.word-press.com/2010/04/21/t-is-for-translation/

Understood: For Learning and Attention Issues. (2017). *Types of issues.* Retrieved from https://www.understood.org

UNICEF. (2016). *Broken dreams: Central American children's dangerous journey to the United States.* Retrieved from https://www.unicef.org/infobycountry/files/UNICEF_Child_Alert_Central_America_2016_report_final(1).pdf

United States Census Bureau. (2010). *School enrollment in the United States: 2010.* Retrieved from: http://www.census.gov/hhes/school/

United States Department of State, Office of Children's Issues. (n.d.). *Intercountry adoption statistics.* Retrieved from https://travel.state.gov/content/adoptionsabroad/en/about-us/statistics.html

United States Citizenship and Immigration Services. (2017). *Frequently asked questions.* Retrieved from https://www.uscis.gov/archive/frequently-asked-questions

Westcott, L. (2015, November 29). Here's the process refugees have to go through to enter the U.S. Newsweek. Retrieved from http://www.newsweek.com/heres-process-refugees-have-go-through-enter-us-398254

Whitman, M. V., Davis, J. A. & Terry, A. J. (2010). Perceptions of school nurses on the challenges of service provision to ESL students. *Journal of Community Health, 35*(2), 208–213. doi:10.1007/s10900-009-9211-3

Wright, W. E. (2010). *Foundations for teaching English language learners: Research, theory, policy, and practice.* Philadelphia, PA: Carlson Publishing.

Yigsaw, A. (2012). Impact of L1 use in L2 English writing classes. *Ethiopian Journal of Education and Sciences, 8*(1), 11–27.

Zong, J., & Batalova, J. (2017). *Frequently requested statistics on immigrants and immigration in the United States.* Retrieved from https://www.migrationpolicy.org/article/frequently-requested-statistics-immigrants-and-immigration-united-states

Zvoch, K. (2006). Freshmen year dropouts: Interaction between student and school characteristics and student dropout status. *Journal of Education for Students Placed at Risk, 11*(1), 97-117.

Zwiers, J. (2008). *Building academic language: Essential practices for content classrooms.* San Francisco, CA: Jossey-Bass.

Michelle Yzquierdo

Dr. Michelle Yzquierdo has worked as a teacher, instructional specialist and educational program specialist. Her doctoral research focused on the factors contributing to the success of high school immigrant students and she continues researching and presenting on this important topic. The foundation of her experience with ELs stems from her time on a school's new arrival team, where she taught students from various backgrounds, including ELLs and first-year immigrant ELLs. As the child of an immigrant, the teacher of numerous immigrant ELLs, and a researcher, Dr. Yzquierdo has seen first-hand what it takes to support ELLs and immigrant ELLs so they may see success. Dr. Yzquierdo lives in Baytown, Texas, with her husband and her son, Kai.

Three ways to order

{
- **FAX** completed order form with payment information to **(949) 200-4384**
- **PHONE** order information to **(210) 315-7119**
- **ORDER ONLINE** at **www.seidlitzeducation.com**

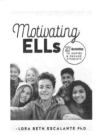

TITLE	PRICE	QTY	TOTAL$
NEW! 7 Steps To a Language-Rich, Interactive **Foreign Language** Classroom	$32.95		
NEW! Boosting Achievement: Reaching Students with Interrupted or Minimal Education	$26.95		
NEW! Motivating ELLs: 27 Activities to Inspire & Engage Students	$26.95		
NEW! Pathways to Greatness for ELL Newcomers: A Comprehensive Guide for Schools & Teachers	$32.95		
NEW! Sheltered Instruction in Texas: Second Language Acquisition Methods for Teachers of ELs	$29.95		
NEW! Talk Read Talk Write: A Practical Routine for Learning in All Content Areas K-12 2ND EDITION	$32.95		
NEW! Teaching Social Studies to ELLs	$24.95		
NEW! Teaching Science to English Learners	$24.95		
NEW! ¡Toma la Palabra! SPANISH	$32.95		
NEW! Mi Cuaderno de Dictado SPANISH	$7.95		
7 Steps to a Language-Rich Interactive Classroom	$29.95		
		COLUMN 1 TOTAL $	

TITLE	PRICE	QTY	TOTAL$
7 Pasos para crear un aula interactiva y rica en lenguaje SPANISH	$29.95		
38 Great Academic Language Builders	$24.95		
Diverse Learner Flip Book	$26.95		
ELLs in Texas: What Teachers Need to Know 2ND EDITION	$34.95		
ELLs in Texas: What Administrators Need to Know 2ND EDITION	$29.95		
ELPS Flip Book	$19.95		
Navigating the ELPS: Using the Standards to Improve Instruction for English Learners	$24.95		
Navigating the ELPS: Math (2nd Edition)	$29.95		
Navigating the ELPS: Science	$29.95		
Navigating the ELPS: Social Studies	$29.95		
Navigating the ELPS: Language Arts and Reading	$34.95		
RTI for ELLs Fold-Out	$16.95		
Vocabulary Now! 44 Strategies All Teachers Can Use	$29.95		
		COLUMN 2 TOTAL $	

Pricing, specifications, and availability subject to change without notice.

SHIPPING 9% of order total, minimum $14.95
5-7 business days to ship. If needed sooner please call for rates.
TAX EXEMPT? please fax a copy of your certificate along with order.

COLUMN 1+2	$
DISCOUNT	$
SHIPPING	$
TAX	$
TOTAL	$

NAME _____

SHIPPING ADDRESS _____ CITY _____ STATE, ZIP _____

PHONE NUMBER _____ EMAIL ADDRESS _____

TO ORDER BY FAX
to **(949) 200-4384**
please complete
credit card info *or*
attach purchase order

☐ Visa ☐ MasterCard ☐ Discover ☐ AMEX

CARD # _____ EXPIRES _____ *mm/yyyy*

SIGNATURE _____ CVV _____ *3- or 4- digit code*

☐ **Purchase Order attached**
please make P.O. out to **Seidlitz Education**

For information about Seidlitz Education products and professional development, please contact us at

(210) 315-7119 | kathy@johnseidlitz.com
56 Via Regalo, San Clemente, CA 92673
www.seidlitzeducation.com

Giving kids the gift of **academic language.**™

REV061419

Three ways to order

- **FAX** completed order form with payment information to **(949) 200-4384**
- **PHONE** order information to **(210) 315-7119**
- **ORDER ONLINE** at **www.seidlitzeducation.com**

Pricing, specifications, and availability subject to change without notice.

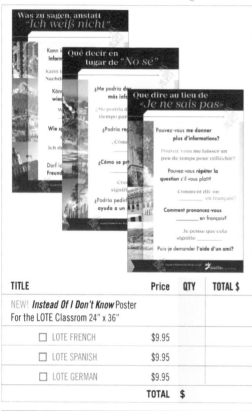

TITLE	Price	QTY	TOTAL $
NEW! *Instead Of I Don't Know* Poster For the LOTE Classrom 24" x 36"			
☐ LOTE FRENCH	$9.95		
☐ LOTE SPANISH	$9.95		
☐ LOTE GERMAN	$9.95		
		TOTAL $	

TITLE	Price	QTY	TOTAL $
Academic Language Cards and Activity Booklet, ENGLISH	$19.95		
Academic Language Cards, SPANISH	$9.95		
		TOTAL $	

TITLE	Price	QTY	TOTAL $
Instead Of I Don't Know Poster, 24" x 36"			
☐ Elementary ENGLISH	$9.95		
☐ Secondary ENGLISH	$9.95		
20 pack *Instead Of I Don't Know* Posters, 11" x 17"			
☐ Elementary ENGLISH	$40.00		
☐ Secondary ENGLISH	$40.00		
Instead Of I Don't Know Poster, 24" x 36" Elementary SPANISH	$9.95		
20 pack *Instead Of I Don't Know* Posters, 11" x 17" Elementary SPANISH	$40.00		
		TOTAL $	

TITLE	Price	QTY	TOTAL $
Please Speak In Complete Sentences Poster 24" x 36"			
☐ ENGLISH ☐ SPANISH	$9.95		
20 pack *Please Speak In Complete Sentences* Posters, 11" x 17"			
☐ ENGLISH ☐ SPANISH	$40.00		
		TOTAL $	

SHIPPING 9% of order total, minimum $14.95 5-7 business days to ship. If needed sooner please call for rates.

TAX EXEMPT? please fax a copy of your certificate along with order.

GRAND TOTAL	$
DISCOUNT	$
SHIPPING	$
TAX	$
FINAL TOTAL	$

NAME

SHIPPING ADDRESS   CITY   STATE, ZIP

PHONE NUMBER   EMAIL ADDRESS

TO ORDER BY FAX to **(949) 200-4384** please complete credit card info *or* attach purchase order

☐ Visa ☐ MasterCard ☐ Discover ☐ AMEX

CARD #   EXPIRES   mm/yyyy

SIGNATURE   CVV

☐ **Purchase Order attached** please make P.O. out to **Seidlitz Education**